I0098823

Spoken for

a book of poems
by
Brian Darnell

This book is dedicated to Meher Baba.

I wish to thank Debbie Finch for her inspiration and support in writing this book. I also wish to thank my brother and publisher, Brent Darnell. This book is also dedicated to my sons, Austin, Caleb and Gus and to my brothers, my mother and late father.

Brian Darnell
July, 2014

Ellora

At Ellora, they started with a stone hillside;
carved out everything that wasn't a temple.

A poem should be like that –
from a vast vocabulary, an eliminating

of words unconnected to one another
until the secret combination is found,

unlocking glimpses of Oneness, the inter-connection.
Words that tremble and hum

when placed together
belong to the realm of the Infinite.

The truth of a poem is in its transparency –
columns of words, sturdy as stone ... clear as glass.

O Lord, take my life. Make a poem from it –
chip away the awkward, the unrelated, the oblique,

the dissonant and obscure. Leave me ...
sturdy, connected, crucial and transparent.

O child of God, the Masters say Truth is not
an acquisition but a paring away of the false.

I love love best

Gratitude roams the ruins of my heart –
the scales have tipped in Your favor.

I've an urge to run through the streets
shouting Your name.

Instead, I kneel and slowly burn.
Dawn bears the same fire on the eastern mullions.

It's not so much that You love me
but that You give me love to give ...

more and more, more and more
and still yet more.

I know nothing of worthiness, except ...
it has everything and nothing to do with love!

O reader! What might we discuss
that you and I don't already know?

Like the elephant in the dark –
everything is true at once!

I love love best as a fire in the chest – silently longing
for the whole house to become ash and cinder.

O child of God, what is there to say?
You are bewildered – inside and out.

Don't circle me

I'm a moth caught on fire.
Don't circle me.

I'm a moon whose silver is stolen from a hidden sun.
Don't circle me.

I'm not the proof. I'm circumstantial evidence.
I'm a dancer who left the ritual

to circle a greater periphery,
to listen to a more distant tune.

The Maypole is back yonder.
Don't circle me.

But, I can stand in the witness chair;
point to the One who made me like this.

I can reflect His gold-red majesty,
the raging furnace of His Being.

I can show the dirty hands that helped
roust Him up the hill to Calvary.

I can point to the Hub, again and again,
standing apart from the spinning crowd

and answer His beneficence
with all the grace, art and passion I can muster.

O child of God, Meher gives you the Light
no darkness can dispel.

Empty bowl

With begging bowl, I roamed the streets,
unaware of the jewel sewn into my garment.

During my last incarceration, You baked me a cake,
folding into the sweet batter a serrated file.

You showed me how my bowl might be used
as a chalice ... or as a ghamela

carting away stones of the wall – by Your grace --
continuously being dismantled between us,

scattering them in the barren fields
from which they came.

Later, You turned the bowl upside down
to wear on my head like a crown;

like Quixote tilting with the windmills.
How great is the jewel of Your compassion!

Each moment the river deposits
it's thick effulgence at the door of my hovel.

I have only to step outside to stake my claim.
I have only to position my bowl under the spigot of God.

O child of God, beware of the illusion of poverty.
Nothing is worth more ... or less ... than your empty bowl.

Goodbye, cruel world!

Holding tightly to Your damaan,
I'm losing my grip on reality.

Serving You and myself ... it's like
straddling two horses at full gallop.

But, in truth, You've given me no choice.
For that I am grateful.

Boxed into a corner, fending off the blows –
You above me, battering me to my knees –

I glance into Your eyes and see ...
Infinite Compassion.

The fight goes out of me.
I'll never again be the man I was.

I've received an inkling of Your love.
Your love – the whole world is drenched in it

as You labor to bring forth
from my recalcitrant body,

the true, the pure, the immutable.
Your love requires two

to slip through the ropes,
One to emerge ... Victorious!

O child of God, bid the world farewell
and see the compassion upon which it is built.

On parting

We wish each other the best ... but, really,
what might we hope for one another?

Our itinerant Lord, from the new life's path,
spoke of hopelessness.

I begin to catch His drift,
many hopes and partings later.

To believe in Benevolence Eternal
is to eschew hope, to shake the dust

from our sandals every step,
tendering the apples of our eyes –

what our Lord tenders ... hopeless love –
not a thought for ourselves ...

or others – hopeless love!
No prayers but praise for the One

whose totality of Love and Mercy
allows not hope's grip nor foothold.

O child of God, timid hearts hope.
The brave-hearted love regardless of outcome.

Where my heart used to be

You left a ruby where my heart used to be.
There's a fire inside that stone.

Now the world is a busy dream
on the periphery of its hard lucidity.

Now its heat and glow
is the gauge of my every endeavor.

The myriad paths of my calculations
peter out into sunlit fields and green woods;

wires cross and sputter; mechanisms derail.
Cause and effect – hoisted on their own petard.

The balladeer is a drunkard and a romantic,
yet, when he stumbles and injures himself,

he remains thoroughly intoxicated,
his Dulcinea ever more pure and wieldy.

Just so, the fire in the stone
draws my prodigal heart –

for what would deter it?
In joy, I burn. In suffering, I burn.

O child of God, nurture the flame within.
This burning is the foot path to liberation.

Confine yourself

O Meher, You confined Yourself –
in the table-cabin, the bamboo cage,

in sundry mountain caves,
in a hut atop Tembi Hill;

in the crypt before ... and after
it became Your Tomb.

You confined Yourself –
in Your great Silence; in a human body.

You confined Yourself
to show how we might be free.

O pilgrim, retire now to the narrow,
holy cell of remembrance;

fetter your mind and tongue
to the unyielding repetition of His name.

Confine yourself to God.
If God is not enough, what is?

O child of God, it's Illusion that's restrictive and tedious.
The Truth of Meher is boundless.

Things that are real

We are forever exchanging words,
my companions and I –

but, rare is the soul who's been willing
to exchange silences with me;

to look me in the eye and enter the realm
where Real things are given and received.

I've been reluctant as well, all of a solitary life,
to trust a human heart – to court that suffering.

That's what I love about You.
You live in that realm.

Even when You stepped down to this turbulent planet,
You brought the beauty of silence with You.

You brought humanity to its gate.
You flooded our souls with its fragrance.

You meet us there yet,
whoever might take Your arm ...

to exchange with Your lovers
the Reality for which there are no words.

O child of God, His advent is an invitation
to join Him in the realm of silence.

Toward a rendezvous

Every moment I'm being ushered
into the presence of the King.

Abducted, heavily cloaked –
the horses gallop, the coach hurtles

toward a predestined rendezvous
across the river.

After millenniums, the tide is turning,
gaining momentum, sweeping everything out to sea.

Our gazes meet as the water swirls
urgently around our ankles.

It matters little now if you are
swept beyond arm's length –

we are bound for the same depths,
our fate sealed, our salvation assured!

In this last measure,
approaching those fabled gates,

I keep you in my heart,
souls interlocked, enfolded ...

into the turbulent embrace
of Arms Everlasting.

O child of God, Love has drenched you to the core.
For such Grace, your life is the only proper barter.

Humility

Your face everywhere at the Center –
a photograph or painting in every room;

from the ethereal beauty of Your younger days
to the silent majesty of the latter.

Seeing Your face, Lord, let my gaze fall
at Your feet – where it belongs;

as I must one day – mind, body and spirit –
fall at Your feet,
to become the dust under Your heels.

Grant me the humility, Lord, to accept myself as I am
by accepting You for Who You are.

Even as my asking is a vain conceit,
I long for the poverty of such humility.

Exhaust my storehouse ... until there's nothing left
that's not a gift from You.

Fill my cellar ... with only Your wine –
that I might share a cup with everyone
who comes to the door.

O child of God, try to love those who you cannot love,
perhaps, beginning with yourself.

The crux of embrace

As its fragrance is hidden in the rose,
my Beloved said,
so My presence is hidden in the human heart.

Under our noses, Lord – unobserved
within ourselves and others.

Only faith and desire keep us daring
the crux of embrace.

Yes, the heart gets tipsy at the first nip
of Your wine – dances in its cage;

deeper in the cup, it grows weepy and ponderous.
And when Your fire sweeps through –

first, a searing pain, then ... burned rubble
from which to look out sheepishly upon the world.

But, You promised us ... You promised Your presence
every moment woven into the heart's delicate fabric

so pervasively, the rose, having never set
tender foot beyond its vast domain,

goes about wailing and weeping
at the absence of its own scent.

O child of God, turn from the world's enticements
to discover within, the fragrance of God.

The darshan moment

Living for tomorrow ...
is a pilgrim in the queue,

absently fingering a garland,
inching his way toward darshan.

Living in the past ... a pilgrim
walking back to the retreat

empty-handed under the stars,
the warmth fading in his chest.

O pilgrim! Live in the darshan moment!
Behind the doors you've burst through,

in the kneeling and bowing moment,
on the floor of cold stone tears.

He awaits you – expects you – every moment,
a cleft of shoulder and neck

in which to hide your crumbling face
and empty your heart; a pillar to lean on,

a gaze from eyes shining
with an unearthly love.

O child of God, live in the darshan moment.
Before and after are the nuances of a listless dream.

Yeswallas

To begin to love, o pilgrim ... stop caring –
what happens, what doesn't happen.

Stop caring what people think;
what you have and have not.

Stop caring who you are,
who you are not.

Stop weighing and measuring,
adding up and sorting out.

Without a scrap of guarantee, the mandali
signed their lives away to enter the New Life,

(the one living eternally ...
even if there is no one to live it.)

At some future station along the road
will the Elder Brother turn and find ...

not another soul upon it? O pilgrim!
Your name is being read out in Mandali Hall!

Will you sit among the Yeswallas?
Or, strike out on a different path ... cross-country,
unmindful and alone?

O child of God, seek the Beloved's pleasure.
As for anything else – stop caring.

Wring and pare

Narrow it down, pilgrim,
to enter the funnel's neck.

Wring and pare, squeeze through ...
the long sliding descent into Ocean.

Your Beloved's hand can only be grasped
this palpable moment

as you sniff the clean scent of Him,
witness His heavenly form.

Climb the path to His humble abode.
He's not there, of course, ... unless you bring Him.

Why not let Him lead you every step from here on out?
(The only sure means of reaching your goal.)

O child of God, pride sustains your insularity.
Companionship is a necessity and an incalculable blessing.

Grace intruded

Grace intruded upon my habitual sorrow
and marked me for its own

like a pattern of ink under the skin,
like an imperfectly minted coin,

a misprinted postage stamp
or a raw diamond selected for its flaws.

Plucked like a flower
for a vase on a bedside table;

like a wild colt culled from the herd –
lassoed, corralled and broken;

like a shell found on the beach
or an injured bird unable to resume
its migratory route,

I left the broad path
for the narrow and the crooked

and now – no path at all …
making my way as everyone must

who tramps toward the gates –
without precedent,

yet, with a Companion who by turns comforts,
inspires, fortifies and illumines the way ahead.

O child of God, Grace is beyond your ken.
To whom much is given much is required.

The prayer of Immensity

I used to crawl through the Universal Prayer
on my hands and knees,

entering through a hatch
in the O before Parvardigar.

By lying flat, twisting myself here and there,
I could inch my way to the last word of worship.

But, one morning, midway through, I tripped
a hidden switch or brushed a secret lever,

or, perhaps ... it was the power of one word
spoken with heartfelt sincerity –

the whole prayer expanded to the dimensions
of the descriptions within it.

Not just the firmament and the depths,
but on all planes and beyond ...

the three worlds and beyond ...
the source of Truth, the Ocean of Love,

beyond and beyond and still yet beyond ...
time and space, imagination and conception.

I found myself in an endless void as the words
of the prayer rose to my lips and faded in my ears.

O child of God, this is the prayer of Immensity –
the Immeasurable, the Unnamable and Incomprehensible.

O child of God, recite faithfully the Universal Prayer.
It's about you and who you really are.

The tending of the fire

There's a fire in the flesh
that must be tended to

and a fire in the wine and a glint of fire
in the ruby of the heart.

Wine's fire enough, in time,
will sodden and subdue the fiery flesh;

the heart's ruby steady the drunken gait
and become a lamp unto the path.

But, o child, when the glint in the heart's stone,
(by the Master's grace), flares and flames,

honor and nurture this fire –
anything you are called upon to do,

anything that can be done.
This fire is the beginning of revelation
and the path home,

the ancient, scattered remnant
lighting our way inward
towards the Source and the Goal.

O child of God, the appearance of fire is grace
and, also, grace – the tending of the fire.

Lost trains

The beekeeper moves the queen;
the other bees circle, swarm, cleave and cling.

Just so, o child, attach your thoughts to the Master
with great and exclusive fervor

until all scattered whims, loose ends,
doubts and desires, all lost trains,

projections, slips and lapses, all indulgent
vagaries and presumptive notions

cluster, coalesce and adhere
to the one true purpose of your existence –

service and allegiance to your Lord –
toiling on His behalf,

striking the spike's head every moment,
again and again and again,

deeply driven and authentic. O child!
Such a clear-headed, harmonious

and vital industry from you
will offer this vapid world

an unparalleled sweetness –
untainted, lucent and gloriously rich.

O child of God, in their turbulent stream, which thoughts
are more valuable than thoughts of God?

The bruising rose

You told the story of an innocent woman
accused of adultery –
tied to a post in the marketplace,

everyone who passed required by law
to cast a stone or some filth upon her ...

which she endured with a noble dignity;
her daughter was brought forth, throwing

not a stone nor filth but, a simple rose ...
and the mother shrieked in agony
as it brushed her cheek.

Let he who is without sin cast the first stone,
You told the crowd in another marketplace.

You, of course, could have cast that stone,
but You have come down, bound Yourself

among the stones and filth
of our marketplaces to endure unjustly

the fateful punishments of being human
and to weigh in Your innocent hands

the culpability of each stone-and-rose-wielding
patron, each laboring, fearful heart.

O child of God, the Beloved is ever merciful.
Protect Him from the bruising rose of your infidelity.

I choose angels

I began to hear a silvery, tinkling sound
occasionally in my left ear – tiny bells ...

delicate as if they grace
the anklets and bracelets

of angels hovering near my shoulder.
Their music makes me smile.

Tinnitus – the audiologist diagnosed.
What does *he* know?

I choose angels.
Sent by You to awaken

and remind me of Your holy Presence.
The commonplace mistaken for Your handiwork?

If I could mistake everything for You ...
I'd be that much nearer the Truth.

If I could hear angels everywhere –
I would discover You ... where You always are.

Haven't we repeated it endlessly?
Everywhere ... and in everything ....

O child of God, the worth of anything is determined
by how much closer it brings you to the Beloved.

finding grace

Mehera asked, years ago, why You chose
so barren a place for Your ashram

(and Your Tomb) ... landscape of dust
and thorns; scorpions, cobras and kraits.

Then, My lovers, You said,
will come only for Me ... nothing else.

These days, You've turned
much of my world into dust and thorns --

a bleak, prickly terrain
devoid of sustenance and satiation,

rife with scrapes, stings and venom,
so that each day, I show up ... only for You

and when side-tracked, return ... only to You,
as the friendly ground shrivels

and the periphery grows wilder,
more and more, finding grace

in the isolation and disparity,
in eccentricity, disillusionment and despair.

O child of God, rejoice when your life becomes a Tomb
in the desolate region of a strange land.

An angel-less God

Into the snowdrift I fall backwards
to make an angel, but ...

gazing upon an endless sky –
the stars' glitter,

the moon's silent shifting,
cold earth against my back,

I feel suddenly under the thumb
of an angel-less God,

overwhelmed by the travails
and duration of my soul's exile

and how many more
arduous journeys stretch before me

'til the promised quenching, rest and reunion.
Then, ... You hoist me to my feet.

God's shape, You say, *is **this** shape* –
pointing to the impression

my body has left in the snow. O pilgrim!
Your portion of infinity spans but fingertip to fingertip;

the duration of your vigil measured
by the heart's brief, pattering flurry.

Union may be far away but God is close at hand –
nearer than your own breath.

O child of God, surely angels hover everywhere
in the realm of Benevolence Eternal.

The brash parrot

Inside a cage of bones, the brash parrot
waddles on its perch, a voluble green flame

shrieking and squalling, much to the delight of some
and, to others, dismay ... for so addled

and vulgar a creature to be declaiming,
in shrill mimicry, the Master's wisdom.

But, those who consider the parrot's words
mere exploitation, fail to grasp the true stature

of its wee, clamoring heart
which, from the first encounter, registered

the import and majesty of the Master's words
and forthwith caught fire, dedicating

its rather ludicrous, inadequate
apparatus of being to the continuous praise

and celebration of the Master's perfect Truth
to anyone who will listen. The particulars

the parrot may not fathom but the great gist
of the tale, its heart knows and owns ... and tirelessly repeats.

O child of God, speak with the impeccable authority
of your own unshakable faith in Meher Baba.

Cabbage leaves

Under a cabbage leaf, Father said
and the son believed him.

He loves me too much,
the child reasoned, *to tell a lie* –

rousing the wonder of a rimy, autumn garden,
naked infant curled among the stalks and stems.

Thumbing now through God Speaks
and other unspoken words You left behind,

I wonder how many cabbage leaves
are enfolded among the bright pages.

Not that it matters.
It was never about hard facts with You ...

but the gentle whisperings and gestures
of a son's trust in his father, a father's love for his son.

Inscrutable tales that quench,
yet prod and fire the groping soul

towards the coming of age,
when mind and tongue shall be stilled –

when Truth shall thoroughly own the man
and the child shall be no more.

O child of God, trust in the love of Meher
where all contradictions are reconciled.

The fire and the rose

Eliot, a contemporary of Yours,
quoting Julian of Norwich –

And all manner of thing shall be well
(adding) -- *when ... the fire and the rose are one.*

Getting into the rhythm of darshan,
flame of garland about Your throat,

like the pulling of oars,
the snaking queue

and the giving, the giving, the giving
in the heat and dust,

skin golden, sadra translucent;
the sea of fire and the lonely swimmer –

no shore visible in any direction ...
and the rose of perfection,

the flame of longing – a culmination,
a melding in the heart's furnace,

intersected and resurrected
in the body and being of the Godman

... and all shall be well
and all manner of thing shall be well.

O child of God, bewilderment, (*literally* – led
into the wilds) is a rare gift from Father to child.

Awaiting

This attempted leaving of myself,
journeying inward;

down the rough-hewn passageways,
bearing the torch;

shaping and paring the heart;
genuflection; dissolution,

the chastening of the flesh,
narrowing of the gaze,

brooking of the burden,
elevating the chin,

erecting the spine;
harboring and dwelling within,

tending the fire; awaiting
His gaze and grace.

O child of God, silence and exaltation,
by turns.

A hint of why

The Ocean has come again ...
to tell us we are not adrift;

more like a river, running towards
and away, of urgency and purpose;

the Ocean has come again ...
to tell us we are not islands –

embracing, sighs and gazes,
the wiping away of tears.

The Ocean, labyrinths
of Love and endeavor,

vast, breathless depths,
come again

to tell us we have no shore,
strongest evidence to the contrary;

no beginning nor end; enemies
and companions – our very own Self.

The Ocean has come again ...
to tell us our loneliness

is but a bitter-tinged drop
in the immeasurable loneliness of God.

O child of God, such an import offers a hint
of why Meher lived in silence.

God's long shadow

Do not make the dead unhappy,
Baba scolded, *by your weeping and wailing.*

Another journey awaits us, o pilgrim,
through the broken gate, the unkempt garden.

Death walks this fine morning in God's
long shadow – efficient, indefatigable servant.

Even Jesus died and those He detached
from Death's arm, soon returned,

dutifully to resume their coupled trailing
through the lily-rucked garden,

the rank and dew-drenched garden –
the body of Jamshed

arranged in the Tower of Silence
and the Master distributing sweet laddoos.

O pilgrim, loosen your grip on the flesh
long before Death offers his arm,

while Beauty's ghosts yet linger,
where the apparent loss shall be suffered.

Jamshed was my brother, Meher averred,
*but I am **Jam Sheth** –* Death's Master.
Death has brought Jamshed to Me.

O child of God, living is dying by loving.
Only the truly dead are beyond Death's grasp.

Spoken for

Love, You say, asks no questions.
My heart's not yet speechless

but, my mind's onto the truth
that all questions lose their validity

this side of the veil. To ask is to break
the silent bond. It's not about believing

or *not* believing, but about love ...
or, not loving and the longing

that's always there
and the despair that inhabits

every laugh and stride and smile,
every social nuance, as we bide our time,

do what we must, granting solace,
here and there, to ourselves and the world

far from the Avatar and the key.
Though, we are lost, we are in His hands,

and *that* is all the difference ...
and that is *all* the difference.

O child of God, why keep speaking?
You are already spoken for.

The hunger

After the poem, comes an emptiness,
a missed opportunity, a haunting plea --

what have you done for me lately?
Emptiness, the Source of poetry;

the ache for God,
the empowerment of every word.

Consult your dictionary
I can't keep writing forever

and what would it mean?
Redemption is not contained in words.

This poem – another brief
and partial realization –

to write it down is to lose it –
unreal when put into rhyme ...

but, that's the job I've been given to save my soul.
And this seems like the end of the poem, so ...

what to do now?
The hunger's still there.

O child of God, be grateful for that hunger.
It will one day lead you to God.

The prayer

The praying is the prayer – not pleadings nor praise.
The *heart's* articulacy is the prayer;

kneeling ... and the folding of hands.
Our nakedness and need is the prayer –

from that first disintegrating morning,
ages past, 'til this evening's calm, gathering dusk,

our nakedness and need is the prayer ...
but, o pilgrims, only a handful ...

the truest heroes of our farthest-fetched tales
ever dare quiet their souls

long enough to listen for God's reply –
to risk hearing the answer

roll across God's vast dominion
or, well up, unsheltered, in the hollows of the heart;

to risk hearing not the Word nor Silence,
but a terrifying, unequivocal Absence.

O child of God, risk all for the courage
to learn the truth of God's love.

Digging our own graves

Everyone requested an official undertaking.
We were issued shovels -- Dig your own graves.

I set diligently about my work, surprised
at the number who ignored the edict.

Or, who abandoned their shovels
at the first backache or blister;

who now pass their days idly.
Some organize workshops and lectures

on the necessity of discernment and the art
of grave-digging. Others dutifully attend.

Distracted by perturbations, desires and moods,
I haven't the suitable discipline for the task

and the ground thick with roots and stones,
but, my shovel seldom lies idle –

that edict is the only instruction I've been given
and I mean to take advantage of it.

I've selected a gravesite far from the commons.
There are others near me, laboring steadily –
graves tidily dug.

We are the eccentrics, our neighbors not quite
grasping the necessity and intensity of our efforts.

O child of God, work for the night is coming.
What's left undone will be added to the morrow.

Make good

All my words hang on a promise I cannot make
and cannot keep – a vanity of imagination,

breath and blood, if the promise has no maker;
if the promise has no keeper.

Shall I continue, o Lord, to tap out
Your timeworn promise on my alphabet board?

Grace, love, salvation – fine sentiments!
but, paper-thin words, and – through my throat –

without substance or luminosity;
indistinct stirrings in the half-light,

the nether-world, the darkness
of ignorance mixed with the darkness of faith;

yet, I praise the promise and the Promise-keeper!
Lord, don't leave me

twisting wordlessly in the wind
at world's end but, gather me sweetly

in Your arms and make good, make good,
make good Your ancient-given promise.

O child of God, what the Beloved requires of you
is faith, forbearance, obedience and attempted artistry.

The garbs of sainthood

The aura wanes; the halo waxes –
no tangible angels, nor saints among us

now that the mandali are gone.
All souls suffer the same ignominy –

our lower-than-angels status;
shame at our nakedness

sans the garbs of sainthood.
In the shadows, we chase

drunkenly after angels,
cherubs in the thickets,

tearfully aware of the heights
from which we've fallen; our souls

not at home in this world, nor in the bodies
of which we are so enamored.

Fear to the soul like pain to the flesh –
something awry ... in need of repair.

The aura wanes; the halo waxes –
a natural evolvement over the aeons.

What makes so painful our short falls
are the selfsame antonymous qualities

we have yet to conquer --
impatience, conceit, distrust and willfulness.

O child of God, perhaps sainthood begins
with the acceptance of our own naked humanity.

Numerous explanations

I should've learned something by now –
how to proceed; which neighborhoods

to avoid, the shortcuts home.
All that beauty crowded into one evening ...

one body ... *one humble gesture*
and I'm thrown out-of-kilter, a grave man

tearful, wishing I might let someone know
but, ... You've seen to that –

there's never anyone to tell;
like the lover's lips ... sealed

so as not to let the smoke escape.
There are numerous explanations for this –

there always are – and I tend to use them,
going down the list ... before succumbing

to the last checked-off square
and ending up alone in my bed

with a book of prayers, exhausted by my own
configurations and convolutions,

wondering why and how I've lived so long
and accumulated such precious little wisdom.

O child of God, where will you hide? Life is
so often too lonely ... or, too lovely to bear.

Hopping a train

Lord, grant me a quick burst
versus the slow gain

of speed in the short window,
muscles versus steam,

hand on the handrail, eyeing the narrow
wrought iron steps; with long hapless strides,

a blast of the whistle, a fire in the chest,
a loose strain on the body, not knowing what waits

if I can haul myself aboard – just knowing,
I don't want to be here anymore

and this train is pulling out.
Lord, grant me the strength,

picturing You somewhere
in a third class compartment

surrounded by the mandali and aware
of my efforts, yearnings and despair;

aware of and awaiting my *fait accompli*.
I've got fingers 'round the jolting

rail of my salvation, as the train
pulls cumbrously, inexorably away.

O child of God, to join the New Life
you must leave behind the old life.

Enter the desert

Enter the desert a wanderer,
uncharted among the dunes,

under the stars; shaped by pressures
only hinted at, half-guessed,

gestured toward; suitable to your nature,
without respite, witness or glamour –

to be a lover is to go it alone.
Swaying upon the bridge, the temptress sings;

the sculptor at the monolith, hewing away.
Caught up in a terrible game of words,

the poet grapples for whatever
endurable term might bare

a slice of the loneliness
that constitutes a human heart.

Hewing away at it ... alone –
that's what we are

and the truth of that
is the truth of God

to be elaborated upon,
the one and only Truth – God alone exists.

O child of God, brave the lonely perils;
seek the truth of the One and Only.

Beads on one string

Abstaining from honey and roots,
leather and silk ... but, that's not it;

five times prayer, the pilgrimage,
no, no. Not the bread and wine

nor a grain of rice per day;
not a mustard seed; not mortification;

not abstinence; not indivisibility
nor devas and demigods ... that's not it;

not brotherly love nor pacifism,
not the Trinity nor the One; not faith, hope, charity;

not servitude nor mastery ... not that, not that;
not the ark, the grail, the ka'aba, the holy texts,

not the Silence nor the Word,
not practices nor disciplines,

ceremonies nor performances, no ... that's not it.
It's not ... it's not.

God can reach around any corner, at any time,
and pull from the rubble a lover, a seeker, a saint.

At some juncture, to adhere is to fall away; to follow
is to fall behind – the path requiring, at times,

abandonment of the path, faith – the leaving of the fold
and fidelity – the incoherent ravings of an infidel.

O child of God, put your faith in perplexity;
find God by renouncing everything you know.

The inconvenience of words

Shambles. My life is in shambles.
You give a wink – now we may begin,

shambling together toward a new goal.
Speak only when spoken to –

the Silent One advises.
And, of what you hear –

take it on faith ... until you finally
abandon that faith for a larger one.

Truth doesn't come in bright boxes;
love doesn't come entombed in the flesh;

happiness is not met demands,
nor sorrows avoided.

It's not peace instead of pain but ...
surrender ... instead of ... everything ... else.

Shambles lead to more shambles,
shambles upon shambles until

an island emerges ... in this life or another,
the tongue, ear and brain growing lax

and truth spoken/heard
beyond the inconvenience of words.

O child of God, no pouring of new wine into old skins,
nor the building of a new house on a rotting foundation.

Common rain

Umbrellas exist so we might not
be caught in an inconvenient downpour;

common, obdurate rain;
the intruder, trouble-maker,

never on anyone's schedule –
cursed and avoided, endured or waited out.

Indiscriminately, it falls, rain,
essential, God-sent. Rare is the soul

who with outstretched and embracing
arms, patience and wonder,

with upturned face submits
to the merciless, unmindful rain.

If we could surrender to the rain,
we could surrender to God Himself

and our long journey
through its motions of stream and cloud,

sun and shower would come quietly
and mercifully to an end.

O child of God, rain falls commonly upon sinner and saint,
lover and infidel, the lost and the retrieved.

Those human years

You became the Word and observed silence,
vowing the whole of Your advent

and adventure Your silence to break but,
all those human years, You held Your tongue.

Perhaps, Your silence was broken
when the Word was broken

and Your bones, like hatchets,
were buried under a stone on a hilltop

made sacred by Your sandal prints,
silence and sweat, or, as Eruch suggested –

You broke Your silence, even as You kept it
which would explain the multitudes

who turned up at Your door,
who answered and, still yet, answer

Your call – Come all unto Me.
You became the Word and that was the answer

and the breaking of Your silence,
at the same moment, the reply

to God's original inquiry and to the heart's
continuous suffering, a reciprocal answer

assuring us we are not alone
in our silence and in our solitude.

O child of God, listen for God's answer and,
failing to hear it, His thundering, silent Affirmation.

On Center

A novel is not a depiction of reality
but, of reality charged with purpose.

Being on Center is like that.
No one enters casually its gates,

nor offhandedly empties out
onto the busy highway beyond;

no chance encounters nor random exchanges
and, around every corner –

infinite possibilities and yet ...
inevitable occurrences

charged with purpose and revelation;
hurtling towards a rendezvous

along the winding footpaths, within
the small cabins, the communal kitchens,

charged with purpose and beauty, nothing
left to chance, nurtured and arranged long ago –

and the invited drop in
and the uninvited hurry past

the pristine and infinite possibilities of such a place
built with love and responded to by Love Itself.

O child of God, home is where the heart is. Hurry,
every chance you get, to His home in the west.

Bowing down

When a saint shuts and opens his eyes,
it's an involuntary bowing down

to the Lord of his heart;
his every breath a prayer;

his heartbeat a drumbeat,
his pulsing blood a trumpeting

of the Spirit's emergence
from the tangle of muscle,

blood and bone of brain and body.
Involuntary, because a saint

has foregone
determinations and judgments ...

left behind faith itself, grasping
the hem of Reality and responding

the only way allowed him – annihilation ...
and – while in the body -- servitude;

bound by vows no longer
made in ignorance but, bound

deep in the body no longer his own,
to obeisance and praise,

to obeisance and praise, to obeisance
and praise to the boundless One.

O child of God, bow until bowing becomes
involuntary, intrinsic to your being.

In His name

In His name we shall gather
on the Hill and sundry places

for arti and prayer. On His Centers
around the world for fellowship,

praise and song, we shall gather.
But, in whose name – jai Baba –

shall another bead be strung?
In whose name – jai Baba –

shall we distinguish ourselves –
exclude, disparage and dismiss?

The name given to us being, simply, His lovers;
The name given to Him being, simply, Father.

O children of Meher!
Gather unto Him now

in the afterglow, before the gathering winds
of ignorance and avarice,

pride and vanity drown out
the lingering melody of His name

and mitigate much of the work
He completed one hundred percent.

O child of God, in His name gather
to celebrate His legacy of Love Universal.

The cross is always waiting

People say he's a dead ringer for Jesus of Nazareth
but, like Mary's spouse, he's just a regular joe,

God taking him aside one day
and laying the Truth on him –

You must bear the cross
all the way to Golgotha ... lie naked there

on the rugged timbers, stretch out your body
to endure the spikes and thorns,

the spear's thrust, the bitter gall.
You may tarry ... and stray along the way –

though, I assure you there's nothing
but pain on either side –

and even lay down your cross, at times;
wander hither and yon, wherever you will,

but know that the cross is always waiting
to be taken up, fitting snugly onto your shoulder.

The cross will not be done with you
until you are done with it –

riding it high on a hill,
angel-accompanied,

pell-mell into the cloud-concealed
and far-flung regions of heaven.

O child of God, open yourself to the terrible
mystery of annihilation and surrender.

Pilgrimage awaits

Pilgrimage awaits and begins
but, you'd rather linger over the back fence

gossiping with neighbors and, after nightfall,
study the erotic silhouettes

on the pulled-down shades, taking note
of the local comings and goings

and the garden needs tending ...
and the daily paper ... the shrubs sculpted,

the lawn trimmed. Pilgrimage awaits
and begins just down the road

but, your house is crowded with characters
and plot devices of your own choosing,

your footsteps heavy on the well-worn boards
as you move from room to room

in a vacant house crowded with characters
behind the curtains, window to window,

door to breezeway, pillar to post with your number
pasted on it as the traffic drifts by out front

in the street which leads to the open road
where pilgrimage awaits and begins if ever

you are moved to vacate the premises
of countless distractions and entertainments.

O child of God, take up arms against yourself.
Surrender has nothing to do with passivity.

The gum of zikr

Erase yourself or help out
by letting go the string

that conducts the tinny voice
of childhood and your subsequent stages'

accumulated impressions, moods
and prejudices to the living moment,

constituting the pernicious illusion
of who you were, are and will be;

sever the continuity of personal history
from the objective present, turning

towards the image and/or
name of the Beloved, refusing to enable,

from moment to moment,
that ghost of a mischief-maker,

letting it drift away like a lost kite,
evanesce into an ethereal sky,

amounting to the nothingness
it always was and always is,

letting go of the string,
letting go of the string,

letting go again and again
and still yet again of the string.

O child of God, take up the gum of zikr
and rub yourself out.

Your brightly lit windows

I became a seeker not knowing
the immensity of the search;

unaware it was myself I had lost.
An inquisitor, a thousand questions

lying under my tongue. You say,
Love ask no questions,

but my love is ever trembling on the lips,
rapping on the windows. My love

is desperate to break into the house
where Your love resides. My love asks ...

for a deeper communion,
an unencumbered embrace, for the complete

torpedoing of my facile buoyancy.
My love asks for dissolution

and dispersal – not into debris,
but into wholeness and holiness,

into whatever it is I have glimpsed
through Your brightly lit windows.

O child of God, ask for love that seals
the lips and turns the heart to ashes.

To Whom I write

Sometimes, I lose track of my soul
writing this poetry, believing words

are the goal and for others
I'm spilling (like blood from a vein)

ink upon the page, but I'm reminded
at the heel of every missive –

O child of God – to Whom I write
and to whose benefit I pursue

this circuitous alchemy of words.
Lord, You leave me no choice –

by that I am ever tormented
and for that I'm ever grateful.

You keep shutting the door
to any possibility of another life.

Hewing it down, accompanying me
in my worldly pursuit, as I sort

through the muddled vagaries of Illusion,
renounce the false and cling to the true

and, among the history of seekers,
renowned and anonymous, take my place.

O child of God, there are only two – child
and Father – until there is only One.

Blue ribbons

... to lose one's life (You say) *is to die by inches.*
And here I am having sprung another leak,

soaking red the bed sheet torn into strips,
lured again by the barker's pitch

and the bawdy wink, swept away
by the ignorant tides, the grinder's wheel

and the smell of sweat. She'll guess
my weight and age, the painted lady offers.

Why ... I'm a featherweight
and as old as the stars; circling

the tawdry midway, fooled again
by the bright lights, the weighted targets,

the crooked scales; by the rhinestones,
the smoke, the make-up and mirrors.

The admission is free into this carnie world
erected in the middle of a cow pasture

where two state highways cross
and disappear in opposite directions.

But, you have to pay to get out
and I can't come up with the fee

having gambled away all my money
on teddy bears and goldfish and shiny blue ribbons.

O child of God, to lose one's life is to die by inches
on the immeasurable path back to your original abode.

The down payment

If you become a world leader,
the eyes of the multitude will be upon you.

If you follow God, few will notice ...
as you slip from the paved road

onto the rough shoulder and into the woods.
You'll go in alone and deep

and no one will follow. This poem
is not for the multitude,

who do not care to hear it.
And if it reaches no one,

my reward will be none the less.
The down payment is sufficient –

an affirmation and a re-phrasing of the promise;
an affirmation ... and a reiteration of the promise.

O child of God, prepare for a lonely journey.
Whoever goes to God goes alone.

The great pretender

For many years His confidant,
His personal attendant, interpreter;

His servant and His companion. Now, Eruch,
some declare you were God-realized all along.

Veiled to your own perfection, some say.
Others claim you were the great pretender

having fooled all the world
but for your Master and a few others.

These conjectures, earnestly asserted,
are meant to invoke awe and reverence for you.

I have no way to judge your status.
But, the man I briefly met –

on Meherazad days
scattered over several pilgrimages,

I admired and revered
not for his mastery, but for his servitude;

for his humanity, not his perfection;
his sincerity, not his cleverness;

for his ordinariness, his utter lack of pretension –
not his ability to pull off an elaborate pretense.

O child of God, as Eruch would advise -- look beyond
Eruch ... to the Godman he so artfully served.

Things I do not know

So this is how it is ... and how it should be.
Other possibilities, potentialities do not exist.

This yearning, this bewilderment –
perfect for me. This suffering, this fear –

infinitely, intricately designed
and fashioned for me alone.

This life I've fallen into, this realm I'm
kicking around in – the perfect kiln for my pottery.

There's no achieving heaven.
Renunciation is not about purification.

No one's handing out gold stars.
Renunciation is about loosening the grip.

Worthiness is won through love
(more and more and still yet more), not effort.

O Lord! Everyone is shouting Your name
and no one knows Who You are!

It's the not-knowing that entices us.
We're sated with the known world.

We're drawn to the interstices, the rends,
the darkness between stars. Who knows?

Maybe I've got it wrong. All my poems
are written about the things I do not know.

O child of God, stop squirming!
Detach; allow; concede; accept; surrender.

The transparency of silence

The other night, I attended a play.
The emcee asked everyone to please

turn off their cell phones. It took me
fifteen minutes to race home and turn off mine.

By the time I got back I had missed
the entire first act. O child of God!

Beware of words! They have a tendency
to become misshapen and entangling,

especially when followed
to their razor-sharp extremes.

Blindly obedient be to the Master, but ...
not to His words. Perhaps, that distinction

is one reason He did not speak, offering instead
the wholeness and transparency of His silence.

Words are for this weighty realm, the known
and the tried. They lose their way entering

the regions of the ethereal and the divine.
Silence – His silence -- is an opportunity

for the heart to exert its authority over words
and over the tireless chattering of the mind.

O child of God, never betray your heart's wisdom
for even the most sacred accumulations of words.

The drunken man

"Aren't you ashamed of yourself?"
the woman asked the drunken man

(who had stumbled and stomped upon her toe).
"Yes," he replied, "... every moment

of every hour of every day."
How to tell serum from pathogen,

elixir from applejack? A shot of whiskey
might prove a bracing tonic for one

but, it's like gasoline on the fire of a raging drunk.
A madman might be slapped and brought

to his senses or, ... sent off on a violent spree.
The Prayer says, *Repent ... for our constant failures*,

but does the evidence add ... then proceed unashamed?
Repent and see yourself ... essence above artifice?

Drowning in shame, what do our inherent
and ever-recurring failures and repentances matter?

What drove the children from the garden? –
their transgressions ... or their disgrace ...

even now enmeshing, riddling with culpability,
the daily machinations of their progeny?

O child of God, keep your head above water
by endlessly repeating the name of your Beloved.

Headed south

It's like standing on the north pole –
every which way I turn, I'm headed south.

Saying Your name is like stacking sandbags
along the river's edge before the expected crest

or, wading afterwards through cornfield rows
flooded chest-deep. It's like

the peal of a bell in a piney woods church
no one attends anymore.

Headed south ... and I can get any color
I want ... as long as it's black.

The river is motionless,
the old man says,

but, the bridge doth flow.
That makes for a rough crossing.

Once I leave the bamboo cage, I am forever
outside of it, headed south; down the hill,

across the tracks, into the open country
of a vast, high, flooded plain.

O child of God, there's only one freedom
and you are countless lifetimes away from its gate.

The heart's sovereignty

Mary of Bethany broke
the alabaster box of spikenard

and anointed Jesus, some of His disciples
grumbling at the expense

but, Jesus said, "She hath wrought a good work .... "
O lover, an imperfection of character

is the desire to be perfect
and a detriment to the path of surrender.

To covet virtue is a sin ...
for covetousness is a sin.

Desire, instead, to be obedient and humble.
Non-attachment is the back road to perfection.

Desire for perfection leads through a labyrinth
of pride, shame and self-involvement

while acceptance of imperfection
constitutes a stirring turn toward surrender.

O lover, spill innocently, like Mary,
the precious oil, anoint the head of Jesus

and be marked forever as a lover
and loyal subject of the heart's holy sovereignty.

Betting on prayer

I grew up impoverished.
After many years, I noticed

innumerable jewels
lay scattered at my feet.

Yet, I remained poor ... because,
I refused to take off my boxing gloves

long enough to scoop them up. So ...
years later –

with great effort and daring –
I took off the gloves.

Yet, I remain poor ... because,
most of the jewels proved to be paste.

Now ... my naked heart and hands
are folded in prayer, which may, also,

be mostly paste -- we shall see –
but, what great treasure

has a poor man to lose anyway ...
betting on prayer?

O child of God, veils within and without
obscure the treasure of infinite worth.

Good news

The good news is –
God supplies our every need.

The bad news is –
sometimes, we need deprivation,

heartache, grief ... failure, pain. O lovers!
I don't know what I am talking about!

But, I keep talking ... because somebody
is putting words into my mouth

and if I can't trust that somebody
then, who can I trust?

So ... I let it ride – all or nothing –
the spinning wheel and the bouncing ball

and this is my path –
sure of nothing, steeped in the lore,

living off the tantalizing possibilities
and the blessed assurance

the goal has already been won,
in fact, the journey has never begun

and here we are again –
playing God's game.

O child of God, rejoice –
playing your role in God's game.

The blade of remembrance

First, it merely pares away
the unwanted debris,

holding your heart hostage –
until ... it tosses you into the street –

down which you wander
out into the wilderness

where it becomes an implement
to scale and explore

the vaulting edifice,
to gain a hand or foothold

in the scattered veins and crevices,
scrambling along the daunting face.

But, it's employed
more opportunely later –

sunk deeply into the chest ...
to strike a vein, to plunder the treasure

deeper than the heart,
whittling one's self to a straw,

for the narrow, twisted passageways
within a vast, interior territory.

O child of God, let His name remind you of the nature
of the dream appearing continuously before your eyes.

Whatever truth or ruse

You once placated the mast Mohammed
with a ruse – the posing of a village woman

as his long-abandoned wife –
to salvage his faith in You,

saying of the mast afterward,
"He's like a child. Unless you

become like a child,
you cannot enter the Path."

O Father of Mercy, I am Your child,
ready to accept whatever truth or ruse

You offer to prod and goad,
undermine and coerce,

reward and punish – to channel me
through the gate without a quiver,

equivocation or turning back.
Whatever truth or ruse will do the trick,

peeling me away from the false self,
this entrancing realm of Illusion;

entering with me into that holistic region
for which You are a living witness, an example of,

where nothing is false;
where everything is true.

O child of God, believe in the One Who spent
every moment of His life leading you toward the goal.

Joy in the pain

It happened again – the path ...
disappeared beneath my feet.

Where is there to stand
in this ephemeral, illusory world?

No solidity, no weight –
no purpose or meaning.

Then, why not float through, my Lord asks,
light and free as a feather?

Because of the pain, I answer.
There's joy – but, always, pain.

There is pain even in the joy ...
but never ... joy in the pain.

That's why I've come, my Lord said.
To bring you joy in the pain.

O child of God, live for your Beloved
and become the purpose you seek.

Your silent veracity

Images and portraits flow
from Your hands through the medium

of silence to further impress,
expose and illustrate the emptiness

of the dream itself ... yet, still I am moving
toward another silence,

down to the stems and seeds,
pulling on the same dry teat,

trusting to the flesh of the heart
and other charlatans and infidels

(being merely human) clustered
around the solitary, lonely point of self.

Lessons in the blood,
(I've spent lifetimes learning) –

the tongues of sham and pretence,
the conceit of fantasy far from truth,

the ineffectual cry and hue of the world –
Your eloquence evoked for some

forty-four years in exquisite silence –
but, are, these latter years, more acutely binding,

razor-sharp, glaringly apparent in the light of Your beauty,
purity, holiness and Your ceaseless, silent veracity.

O child of God, as Truth is beyond words,
so Illusion is beyond substance and sustenance.

Fishes and loaves

It's not like baking bread
from granny's recipe or, shaping

and assembling furniture.
It's more like the tracking of a deer

or ... catching a fish – the application
of a randomly accumulated expertise –

recognizing favorable conditions,
combing likely environs.

It's like the setting of a hook,
the ensuing improvisation,

gauging the familiar give and take
before landing the prize.

And then, ... maybe, offering it to the fisher of men,
Who, along with some of those methodically

baked loaves, may use it to feed the multitudes ...
or, maybe, not. It's no concern of mine,

lying belly full on a hillside, drowsy with wine,
my allotment taken off the top,

my Beloved's form in full view,
His voice a sweetness in my ears.

O child of God, be ever vigilant for bread, wine
and that sudden, sharp tug upon the line.

The silent Christ

The silent Christ spoke only with His eyes –
hanged from an invisible cross.

His sheep not scattered but, becoming lions
and dragons, becoming torches

roaming the night. The silent Christ
marveled at the intricacies of His own effort

and the trouble God took for just one Word.
Spoke with His eyes ... His blood, bones,

heart and brain to call forth loudly
His children from the wilderness

which has enveloped them
to His table of bread and wine.

The silent Christ lies in sweet repose
as the hue and cry of the world echoes

and fades around Him, His work completed
one hundred percent, His silence going about now,

methodically, drowning out
the blasphemies of the world.

O child of God, be silent yourself. Don't speak
of things you know so very little about.

Borrowed clay

There's a path which must be walked.
There's no choice about it; no turning back.

A footbridge to be crossed –
high, narrow, pendulous; a candle

held before the chest, cupped hand
and cautious steps protecting its flame.

In the heart, there's a wine cup, brimful,
to be balanced precisely

lest a drop spills in vain. There's a prayer –
heartfelt, word for word -- which must be said

as the candle is protected
and the cup is balanced;

a silence to be kept intact
as the prayer is recited

and the cup is balanced,
the candle protected –

a silence pure, immense as the silence
Meher left after returning the borrowed clay.

And there are various outward, karmic circumstances
which must come together like stars

in alignment and agreement. Footbridge, candle,
wine cup, prayer, silence, stars and circumstance ....

O child of God, there is more to the path
the farther along you go.

The great Story-teller

The autobiography is true enough
but, the main character doesn't exist;

has never existed. The reader completes
each page, rips it from the book,

crumples it up and throws it into the fire.
The poet is the invention, not the poem

spilling out onto the page –
existing only by the footing

or handhold acquired between
rhythms and rhymes.

The poet is silence itself, far away ...
yet, embodied in phrasing and imagery.

It's the story which has a life of its own,
not the subject or the author.

It's the poem which is closer to the truth –
the mere whimsy of a gossamer dream

composed by the great Story-teller
for His own gratification and amusement.

O child of God, why do you writhe in torment?
Why struggle to change that which does not exist?

Stained by hope

We stand and pray – *O Parvardigar* ...
with folded hands, quaking hearts

and all the faith and hope
we can muster.

We stand and pray and You say
we must shed our hope –

which leaves only our naked faith.
Preserver and Protector of all ...

we pray because we suffer
vulnerability and *impermanence*

and You say our faith is stained
and diluted by our hope.

Yes, (I accept that) but, (for me) –
not in God. My hope and faith is in You.

In the life You gave the world.
I take You at Your Word;

say the prayers *You* participated in.
There are no other words left to me

which give *more* than their meaning --
which give solace and faith and *hope*.

O child of God, stand before your Father;
say the prayers, naked and honest as you dare.

Journeyman's cloak

Long you have wandered the desert.
Enter now the palace of the King.

His only requirement –
remove your filthy coat.

Possessions, He does not demand,
nor the servitude of your body;

nor must the torch of your wisdom
and awareness be extinguished.

He demands only ... that illusory cloak
to which you so fanatically cling, be shed –

your journeyman's cloak,
ragged, encrusted, malodorous –

cloak of foreign alliance, of feigned separation;
cloak of provisional power and false dominion.

The King and the desert await you, pilgrim,
on either hand. It's your decision to make.

O child of God, the bargain was struck ages ago.
Take it now ... or leave it.

The powers that be

My house is lonely tonight.
I step into the backyard –

fenced in, subdivided;
stars fixed above the trees,

the moon turning its cold shoulder.
I feel small, overlooked, left behind

in the vastness .... After a time, I notice
the moon shadows crossing the lawn –

I *am* getting somewhere –
in spite of myself.

The earth turning me, hurtling me
around the sun, also,

on a journey toward its destiny.
I might seem inert, broken down,

stuck in an ineffectual rut but,
eternal forces are ever rushing me,

in their own sweet time, toward a rendezvous.
My choice -- to have faith in the benevolence

of the powers that be ...
or, lack faith ... and despair

as I languish behind the high, sturdy fence
I have erected for myself.

O child of God, don't worry, be happy.
Despair, in any case, will gain you nothing.

Wrens and sparrows

I write my poetry on a crust of bread
I found in the bottom of my pouch,

dropping crumbs along the path
for the wrens and sparrows.

I won't be coming back
this way and no one will follow

into this particular plot of trees.
The woods are deep. I'll write

as long as the light holds out.
God illumines the path

only one step at a time
and my own torch has been thrown down.

It's like a crust of bread –
the moon above the horizon.

My mortal existence is a crust of bread.
This poem is dedicated

to the wrens and sparrows.
I wish I had more to give.

O child of God, venture where there is blitheness
in dissolution; unalloyed bliss in obliteration.

Assortment of blessings

A lover arriving from the west, the end
of her long quest to meet the Beloved.

Tomorrow, You said;
Eruch protesting – she's come so far;

she so wants to see You.
Tomorrow, You said,

she will want to see Me even more.
The assortment of blessings You give

is the longing to see You *even more* –
a fiery, chafing treasure,

at times, requiring You to give nothing ...
or, even, take away.

The treasure You give I squander daily
on the heart's rank strangers –

little or nothing left for the Giver.
You knock upon the door,

waiting to take birth
and are ever turned away –

while on the outskirts, I wait also
having not accumulated enough

seared flesh to purchase the ticket
and be ushered into Your waiting arms.

O child of God, the blessings of your Beloved
are dissimilar to the blessings of the world.

Too much like death

You lived in silence. I can't abide it.
Too much like death. Even while

lying motionless and mute in the casket
You've so lovingly fashioned for me,

my mind is stubbornly shouting blasphemies,
roaming the known parameters.

I climbed in willingly enough.
Made myself comfortable.

I don't regret it.
But, this protracted interment –

is as stylized and boring
as any funeral ever was

and still I haven't the courage
to clamp down the lid long enough

for You to sink the nails.
You came not to teach but to awaken.

Lucky for me – because I never seem to learn.
And, instead of holding on to Your damaan –

being dragged pell-mell into the Infinite-Eternal,
I hold tightly to the ragged shirttail

of this wanton, roaring world; the sad
and flustered illusion of my false self.

O child of God, hold your tongue and let
Meher's silence become your last triumphant shout.

When hearts fail

Gathering my faith to my chest,
tramping toward another fire,

angels hovering not near enough,
perhaps, to smell their lily breaths

but to hear their wings beating the air;
aiming towards my best shot,

a wild and improbable lifeboat,
my Beloved shunting me toward His table –

(if such a table exists among
the misted hopes and myths of men)

by sapping the flavor of every sip and morsel
which does not bear His thumbprint and signature.

Or, am I reading too much into this –
creating for myself a solace,

thin and impalpable as the ghosts
I have long chased,

which routinely plague
all partakers of this reality?

God only knows and He's keeping mum.
Apparently, it's faith He's after in the interim;

faith, in the end, all He leaves, our fallback
connection when hearts fail to love.

O child of God, you belong to Meher Baba.
You couldn't leave Him if you tried.

Pilamai's chair

You threw Pilamai's chair from the moving train
when she refused to occupy it in Your stead.

You revere your feelings of shame, You said,
more than me. Yes, Beloved, more than You,

I revere the shame of my flesh,
the impertinence of my doubts,

the usurpations of my thoughts and will ....
How could it be otherwise?

They are not surrendered already to You.
For that I am deeply ashamed

and cling to my shame and not to You.
The great gulf between us is filled with small things –

the petty, the furtive, the vain and paltry.
What is my life that I should value it?

What would it have been without You?
Dying to shameful desires, I would be Yours

and with You, inseparable, non-dual ...
and other facile attempts at description

of that which the tongue, eye and ear
are incapable of bearing.

O child of God, the Beloved demands absolute
obedience ... for *your* glory, for *your* emancipation.

Never drenched

Everybody's crying 'mercy', Mose Allison wrote,
when they don't know the meaning of the word.

We know only definitions, strategies
and the strained perversities

of God's most dynamic and intrinsic Qualities.
Approached only through hearsay,

conjecture and imagination,
we judge God's love and mercy

and find Him lacking – while it is our own
judging hearts which lack those very virtues –

never drenched, never drenched in the aspects
of infinite, eternal Love and Mercy.

O Meher! You dropped into this dream.
We demanded explanations –

the Ultimate Reality delivered in dream speech;
justified by dream logic; redeemed in dream dynamics.

No wonder You sealed Your lips
against the notion Truth can be taught

and learned ... not realized and lived.
But, here again, I take Your part, my Lord,

against a greater part of the world, offering explanations.
Do I justify You to others ... or to myself?

O child of God, throw yourself over the cliff.
You nor the world have anything of value to lose.

Sum total

Who are you going to believe,
Ramdas asked his disciples,

me ... or your lying eyes? (Or, words
to that effect). Only Kalyan chose the Master,

fetching a lantern for the noonday prayers;
others *wanting* to believe but left stranded

as the ship sailed, grieved and abandoned.
(Only the disinterested ones

certain of the madness of the Master and his minions,
survived unscathed).

It is hard to see the Light; hard to see
the darkness, to put your lips upon the foul

and deadly with no inner assurance
of salvation and sweetness,

the universe bearing unholy witness against you.
An absurd, lonely, desperate risk and quest –

(did He ever describe it otherwise?) –
to go against the sum total of all you've ever known.

O lonely, hopeless seeker of God,
only Meher is there to balance the scales,

only Meher, only Meher inviting you
to join Him in His divine madness.

O child of God, run fetch your lantern!
Follow your Lord into the noonday sun.

Faith is a wooden sword

Faith is a wooden sword.
Take it up, o lover, against the ogres

and demons of your dire imaginings,
which (the Masters say)

is the substance of adversity and suffering
and, yet, which bar the way

to your rendezvous
with Who you really are.

Discipline yourself in the art of war.
Labor for the day

you will be handed a sword of steel.
Faith is a leave-taking

from the worldly ranks, a declaration
of allegiance to the King. O lover,

let your ordinary and inevitable
death and suffering

take on a vital and pointed glory!
Faith is a wooden sword, a testing of the blood.

The *essence* of faith is surrender.
Pure and ultimate faith – surrender ... and victory.

O child of God, take up your sword
and be faithful to the only worthy One.

The atelier door

The canvas is bare
and the base coat is pain,

as we begin our self-portrait,
muting even the sharpest

delineations, the staunchest hues.
We dream of truer colors

until some cry of pain, interior or exterior,
(from ourselves or others),

returns us to the task at hand.
But, soon we shall drift away (once more),

to conjure up another masterpiece,
flitting about the room,

staring from the windows, hovering abstractly
above palette, canvas and easel.

The base coat is pain
and the atelier door

is locked from the outside.
The portrait paints itself – beyond

our judgment, control or critical flair
and we are, alas, (try as we might),

bound inextricably to our labor, yet, unable
to add or subtract a single stroke.

O child of God, the origin of ego is attachment
made manifest through ceaseless imaginings.

The business of love

I love you more
than you could ever love yourself,

Meher Baba said. My self
not in the business of love –

neither payments nor debts;
my self ... the absence of love

and love ... the absence of self.
Looking for love under the street lamp;

in the assorted galleries of fantasies and flight.
Finding none in ourselves, we look to others –

who look to us across the great divide.
The love of which my Lord speaks

offers no barter nor bargain – love not
because of what we might give (or receive)

but, what might empty us, what might
(in our absence) *make room for,*

make room for ... Love,
make room for ... God.

O child of God, what is this business of love?
Meher says it's the essence of your being.

The joy of breath

It's like sewing the torn seam
of a treasured jacket –

needle pushed in, pulled out
to patch the rend that lets the chill in.

You might say His name
with each stroke if you've a mind to

and go through the day
with mercy in your throat;

like a swinging gate awhisper
on well-oiled hinges – you keeping a nearby watch

to chronicle the traffic, follow your thoughts
where you will and leave off

where you must -- stand and observe
the lone traveler disappearing against the sky.

Wherever you end up, the gate will follow,
ready for you to take up your post again.

You won't change much (coming in/going out) –
your deportment, perhaps, discernment,

your rash decisions, easy attachments –
O seamster, name-dropper, sentinel, spy (!),

holy, holy witness, knowing only the *moment*,
inside and out, and the primal joy of breath!

O child of God, will you *ride* the ox or,
chase forever behind its random wanderings?

Where do I go?

Where do I go
to get my innocence back?

O fresh-cheeked, joyous, clear-eyed boy!
Shall I break the news to you?

I sold you out ... ages ago, for shining trifles.
Innocence strewn and squandered,

compliance wheedled and coaxed –
secret indulgences, anonymous compromises,

a whisper and a hope ... and all for love;
all for love ... but, I lacked the courage.

Beaten up, pasted over, trampled under ...
I betrayed you and failed you ...

and here you are again, forgiving me,
begging me to come clean.

I have no promises to make. It will take courage ...
all the courage I never had –

the countless moments of truth
that came and went and found me wanting.

Where do I go ... to find that courage?
To get my innocence back?

Here, said my Beloved.
Come here. Come to Me.

O child of God, your pretenses worn threadbare ...
let your humble, homely truth shine through.

My story

This is my story, this is my song –
praising my Savior all the day long.

Praise, constant praise – deeply in love
with the depths and intricacies of the story,

praise to its Author; receiving
His assurance, most blessed.

Surrender becomes a way of life,
life becomes praise –

walking, talking, living, breathing exaltation!
God created Existence for each *one* of us!

Separately unfolding before our senses.
This is *my* story, my holy moment under the sun.

Accumulated history – merely the backdrop;
the world in periphery – celebrities, royalty,

heads of state, bit players in *my* story.
My incredibly crooked story, *my* off-beat,

out of kilter song, a gift from God!
Awed and humbled, marveling in the joy,

enduring the suffering –
surrender, the one gift I might offer

God in return ... and fetch the closing words,
the last page, the final chapter.

O child of God, love the Story-teller and the story
without attachment to outcomes, trajectories and purpose.

Taken with You

You took me, Lord,
to a place inside myself

where I'd never been before. You took me –
and I've been taken with You ever since.

I picked up a copy of Your book
and I can't put it down, wondering how it turns out,

how all the characters and plot-lines
tie together and reconcile.

You stuck to me like fly paper
to some comedic schmuck

in the silent movies –
making an enraged fool of myself.

I can't pry You loose.
I can't get to the bottom of You.

You took me – and I can't shake You
even as I tremble and waver

and pitch my prodigious fits. You took me –
and I've been taken with You ever since.

O child of God, allow Your Beloved the last dance
and then, ... allow Him to take you home.

Head over heels

To indicate the effect breaking His silence
would have upon the world,

Meher Baba once cupped His hands
to form a globe and then, deftly, flipped it over.

Why shouldn't I believe Him?
Secure within the predictable

and familiar orbits and juxtapositions
of various touchstones and landmarks,

well-accustomed to the daunting pattern
of stars spinning above my head,

the dependable earth beneath my feet,
my Lord, mercifully, upended my world ...

set me upon a path through foreign territory –
everything new, strange and oddly out of whack.

Even today, years later, whenever I come close
to regaining my equilibrium, re-acquiring my bearings,

with a swift sweep of His hand,
He clears the playing board.

He once formed a globe
with His hands and then, flipped it.

Upside down, someone said, interpreting the gesture.
No ..., He wryly corrected. *Right side up!*

O child of God, celebrate the moment you fell
head over heels in love with your Beloved.

The malady of loneliness

Leave me alone with my thoughts,
I heard myself say. Thoughts providing

distractions and entertainments
to keep a rendezvous at bay.

We inhabit, perhaps, the same house
but, lost in thought,

I never cross paths with my Companion,
(evidenced only by wistful glimpses, residual clues).

Am I truly alone within this odd, familiar structure?
Fear keeps me from exploring the premises.

I take, instead, to the streets
or hole myself up in my fiction-lined attic.

I'm free to entertain, of course --
friends in the parlor, spooners on the porch,

lovers in the rooms upstairs, but, to uncover
whether or not I am truly alone,

I must descend into the dank bowels,
near to the crumbling foundations,

and, in that darkling place,
kindle a lonely flame ...

to expose ... or not, the cornered face
of my Beloved, my Companion.

O child of God! For the malady of loneliness,
solitude is the only possible cure.

Savored love

I forgot that Love existed, Morrison growls –
an effort to express the bewilderment,

the essential ineffability of the revelation.
When God reminds you of Who He Is,

no glib retort comes to mind. A cry
of some sort might escape your lips

as your heart tries to leap from your chest.
You wonder how your legs can carry the weight,

if your brain will ever jump back into gear,
when you remember ... when you *remember* ...

when your *heart remembers* – Love exists.
And ... if God is Love, Love is God.

The Almighty, as a concept, might be elusive –
but, we've all savored love

and the deeper we've drawn from the well
the more precious and purer

we've found the water. Debris brushed aside,
the heart begins to flow again

as a living source. When Love is remembered ...
profoundly remembered – existence is bathed anew

in the light and sheen
of pristine Truth and infinite possibilities.

O child of God, again and again we are returned
to our lost and forgotten heritage.

Man of God

I became an adult, in many ways
remaining a child. To fill out the clothes

of a grown man, I stuffed them with straw.
A sturdy cross I constructed

to climb upon and cling to –
to keep myself tall and erect,

lest I be caught out.
The rod and staff of that cross,

binding me to itself, rooting me to one spot,
became my sole comfort and orientation

on this wavering, spinning planet.
But, then, ... Lord, I encountered You

and began to fill out my potentialities.
And now I see,

plainly, the daunting task before me –
O child ... O *man* of God, climb down

from that cross, exchange it for another;
take to the itinerant new life. Come what may

and wherever you might be led, bear
that ancient/new cross. Follow your Elder Brother.

O child of God, Meher has come to awaken in you
that long-dormant, slumbering man of God.

Fly to Him

For those who are Mine, my Beloved said,
I put all their stars and planets

in my cup of tea and drink them up!
Every path and pattern, signpost, scriptures,

bridges, leaves of tea,
the dust at our feet and flung across

the heavens stirred and upended,
sweetened and aligned

by His Presence on earth,
His steady, knowing hand.

Every need, entreaty and prayer
must fly to Him ... must fly to Him,

the Source and Center of our quest –
for the essence and strength of His method,

the core of our salvation
depends upon ... total dependence.

He stirs in His cup our planets
and stars to sweeten His chai,

to spin us tighter still into the web
of His work and our ultimate salvation.

O child of God, drink from the Godman's cup
and taste the rarely-tapped mead of heaven.

Early post-advent

I pray for this poem (which I intend) to be a prayer
trampled in a field of fresh snow,

making sense only
when viewed from a great height;

not merely a shadow of life and death
but, the difference between

solace and grief, hope and despair.
I pray for your poems, too, o lovers of God;

your prayers, too – ink, oils or clay ...
eye, throat, shoulders, thighs.

May you reach that purity of breath,
blood and bone – poetry beyond sound and form;

may your blood run its tireless course
from the moon's blotched surface

to the rich earth beneath the snow
and your bones ... your bones -- may they turn up

in the spring, in green fields,
bleached evidence of fallen soldiers,

lest future lovers fail to recognize us –
an enclave and asylum of poets, comrades,

artists, lovers and seekers of Truth in these mad
and turbulent, early post-advent years of Meher Baba.

O child of God, say your poetry and your prayers
with precisely the same fervor and devotion.

To love

To love God in the most practical way,
Meher Baba said, is to love our fellow beings.

I nod always, mumble under my breath –
yes, because everyone is You.

But, one day, You whispered in return –
because, lover, ... to love ... is to love God.

The sculptor grinds the chisel to a perfect bevel.
The sawyer sharpens the blade's teeth.

The cutting torch, the welder adjusts
to the precise admixture

of acetylene and oxygen.
Now the flame can cut steel.

It is the purity of love that shapes and sharpens
the chisel, the blade, the flame,

allowing for the cutting through,
the paring down, the severing.

O child of God, to love is to teach
the heart how. To love is to love God.

Desire nothing

Desire nothing, You say. But ...
my house is built on desire –

a caravanserai of ceaseless comings
and goings; of compacts, treaties,

agreements and arrangements.
Perhaps, o wanderer, you've left your house

and now haunt the tombs of saints,
study the scriptures, indulge in the sweet

intoxication of prayer; perhaps,
you've renounced worldly indulgences

to take up spiritual indulgences.
Perhaps, you covet love now ...

liberation, peace, paradise ...
the imagined glory

of your own eventual Godhood.
Desire nothing, You say. But ...

my house is a ruin on the side of the highway
travelers tromp through on their way

to presumed important appointments,
thrilling adventures and soul-serving endeavors.

They often invite me along. Even my
entrenchment and intransigency is desire.

O child of God, hold your tongue. Desire nothing ...
because, nothing is withheld.

To have not the heart

The Godman came to give the Word
yet, firmly sealed His mouth to all entreaties.

If you can slice open,
with the very fine blade of surrender,

your heart to that, if you can speak to it
affirmatively with the dry wit of a dust grain

or, add to that great silence, the enduring silence
of a stone then, perhaps, awaiting you, o lover,

(so the Master says) just around the bend,
is the promised Word and the promised Ear.

The Godman came (again) to give hope ...
and to crush hope, to give the law

and to sow the seeds of chaos,
to mend and reconcile, rend and separate,

to empower and eviscerate, instruct and confuse,
to act as one with karma, to reveal the path

and to remove it from our daily thoughts.
O child of God, choose between yourself and God.

Simple as that. Better yet, have not the heart,
nor the strength, to lift a finger of protest or desire.

O child of God, to (possibly) know your Father
is to abandon all hope of understanding.

Your side of the river

These days, often, You back me up
against the river boundary, boxed in ...

so I have to herd my fears – my sensibilities,
rationalities – toward Your inland still waters

and with numerous ginger steps, artless calculations,
make my way back to the heartland, homeland –

open fields, blue skies, peach orchards
and wild persimmons, the fertile soil

and the furrowed ground, the ever-looming
heartaches and pendulous, inherent hopes

and disappointments. I know that other territory well –
across the river, that dark wild which can feel like truth

and the black depths of the exhausted quarries,
their sharp and treacherous angles.

You drive me to the river, these days, and leave me there,
knee deep, to find my own way back. Against Your silence,

my interrogations come up naught, the compromises
all on my side, Your orthodoxy and good graces

evermore far-fetched and unreasonable, as I cling
that much more tightly and praise You for my full cup

on this extraordinary path I reluctantly (at times)
traverse on this, Your side of the river.

O child of God, conviction is a gift of the Master.
Faith, in the interim, is an offering of the lover.

Thin-skinned heart

You say, *Don't try to understand Me.*
Good advice, since You don't

quite make sense, that is to say,
nothing seems to fit ... and You,

of course, are everything
but, every so often You send me off

on an analytical jag, knowing
I'll come back around because ...

my thoughts always lead me in circles.
It's about time, this time;

inevitability and purpose, distance
and proximity and the ubiquitous

reality of non-significance ... while never leaving,
mind You, the confines of my thick skull,

never venturing near the love-strapped,
thin-skinned heart I bear inside ...

until I am, at last, back on Your stoop,
knocking on Your door ... and being let in

graciously, mercifully, as I fall in timeless,
eternal repetition, at the unfathomable,

beyond imagination and conception, illusion
of Your body and Your holy, human feet.

O child of God, one significant allurement of faith
is the lack of any coherent alternative.

The absence of metaphor

Poets love words because
they can push them around

(in an affectionate way), gather and herd,
winnow and cull, shape them as they will,

split them into several, simultaneous meanings.
A stone in the hands of a mason

is merely a stone, to be employed
or rejected. In a poet's hands,

a stone ... might be a human heart,
a biting grief, a planet, a tomb.

Poets have a hard time with God.
With God, a stone has no meaning.

With God, a stone is simply THAT,
as God is THAT, as each moment is THAT,

as a lifetime, an age, an aeon is THAT.
It's the absence of metaphor, of signification,

the absence of meaning combined
with the utter, inviolable truth of everything with God

that leaves the poets ultimately inert and mute ...
that halts their poetry at the threshold of the divine.

O child of God, Meher Baba awaits
with the Word which has no meaning.

Uncut wood

Humble, Lao Tzu advised, as uncut wood.
Too late for most –

we've already carved ourselves up –
rasped and whittled, notched, embedded,

painted and pasted over ...
to make our shape and image

acceptable to the world –
lovable, respectable ... exceptional!

O! The pain involved now
in the slicing through, the paring down

below the acquired ornamentation,
every cut, by our blade, a further disfigurement;

never to reclaim the purity
and authenticity of the original grain.

Weather me, Lord! Over the aeons,
down to the essence – by the elements –

as I cede and acquiesce,
mourn and pray for humility –

not the original, guileless condition –
but the humility of helplessness and futility,

the inability, in this lifetime, to recover
an innocence so irretrievably lost.

O child of God, return to your original state
by the grace and dharma of the Beloved.

Lighting a candle

I saw the Friend
shining in your eyes.

Beheld by His kindness,
my heart and body remembered

the holy companionship
my mind had worn out and misplaced.

I heard my silent Master
in your throat – voice and laughter –

stepping daintily, for a few moments,
outside time's flow.

I felt the touch of the Friend
in the softness of your eyes;

His unwavering good spirits
in the cup of your smile.

Anew, I experienced
the awe and reverence

I had frittered away over the years –
(down to the last scraps and tittles) –

recouped by the posture and demeanor
of your body humbly kneeling before His chair.

Lighting a candle with a candle
in the heart of this late autumn evening.

O child of God, your Beloved comes to you
in countless and ingenious, multifarious ways.

The human source

When I first fell for You ...
what improbable tales You told!

I emptied my quiver in Your direction –
trusting not one smooth line.

I empty my quiver still, because,
these days, I so very much trust

Your benevolence, Your forbearance.
A cipher adrift in the cosmos

or, one orbiting a centric faith –
I recommend the latter. Faith is blind,

yes ... but, I follow the scent –
jasmine and rose – the ocean's roar

and, in my teeth – the taste of blood, salt,
and candy prasad. O Lord!

Perhaps, You are not with me now
as I write this. How could I ever be sure?

But, I trust You – the flesh and form You were,
Your Word, Your mercy, Your munificence.

I trust the awakening
You have evoked in me.

O child of God, make Meher both the godly
and the human source of your faith.

A further roughening

Longing begins when that thin layer of ice
burns the skin down through to muscle and bone.

Strain at the tether long enough,
the strain itself becomes the tether –

looseness binds; delight chafes;
time issues yet a further

tumbling and roughening;
freedom begets a vapid, lonely inertia.

The ache for release, eyes scrubbed by tears,
and the lock's key becomes the fiery ache.

O! Rough and vast is the pitching ocean,
the true course straight and narrow.

I can't hold the wheel. Lord!
I can't hold the wheel! Come!

Lend Your shoulder; apply Your will.
Lord, come. I can't hold the wheel.

O child of God, let barriers and encumbrances
become the means of propulsion and velocity.

Wild tales

Some lovers study the structure –
gnawing the bones through

to the wine-drenched marrow,
while others sink their teeth

into succulent flesh – meat and fruit –
of torch songs, wild tales, ragged breaths;

of torn pages and broken spines, wine
bottles passed mouth to mouth –

eyes shining; beards, breasts, lips, chins
glistening, the holy carpet thoroughly,

irredeemably soaked and stained.
There's room at the cross for everyone

but, a wordsmith's fair warning –
muscle, pulp and fat soon to wither on the rack,

spoil and sour, to the elements returned,
scattered, leaving the corporeal body

to its hardy blades, clubs, cages, pins and flaps;
the fruit to its rinds and seeds, for the scholars

and preachers, priests and theologians
to suck upon, chew and pick over in the age

to come of the estrangement, the diasporas,
the darkness, the trough and the lone wanderings.

O child of God, every lover's path is determined
in precise accordance to the grace of God.

A shared life

The island in the zygote –
floating miniscule and fragile;

island in the womb –
so vulnerable, so vulnerable.

The island in my head – so insubstantial,
so subjective; inside my skin – so mortal;

the island in my chest – so isolated, so lonely.
White dab of sand in the middle

of a dark blue sea until the Ocean Itself
leaves footprints along the shore.

Accustom yourself, its pattern reads,
to a shared life. And for years now,

my island fortress has been shrinking
under the determined elements of truth –

wild winds, brutal storms, the heavy seas.
When every place you trust,

the footprints read, underfoot is gone;
everything you thought solid proven flimsy,

the truth will swim into view –
truth to drown in; truth vast as the Ocean

encircling your sad
and dwindling little island.

O child of God, every man is an island
until reclaimed by the Ocean of Love.

A superior baptism

I'm not the least bit nostalgic
for earlier times You broke the bread

of my body and dipped it
in Your blood red wine;

lit the plaited fuse, soaked the sponge in fire.
What a preposterous creature –

under the influence
of a faith so absolute it couldn't fit

inside my head, my mouth, my body;
a faith – the ocean itself –

in which I swam and breathed.
I don't want to go back down

the way I came. The catch
is this – faith without proof is, perhaps,

a thousand kisses stronger in the clenches,
a barrel full of heady wine; my tears

a superior baptism; my hand above the flame
the needed tempering for a greater joy.

To a green heart, You once gave grace –
jubilant wonder and faith unforced,

its tattered shell and remnants now,
dear and sacred as any proof I might bear.

O child of God, your Father gives what's necessary –
else, the least to the greatest faiths are all in vain.

Hope, sturdy beast

Hopeless, You say, instilling hope
in a pilgrim's heart -- paradise within reach

and power. Hope, sturdy beast of burden,
bearing souls and suffering

toward the gates, must be abandoned,
You say, reinless among the dunes –

a fly in the ointment, oil in the lamp
whose flame prevents our eyes

from growing accustomed to the dark.
Tiny circles of illumination

to which we cling (except where we are –
our shadow deeper than the vastness beyond).

When the desire to know the Truth
pales before ecstatic wonder,

surrender gains a foothold, truth darts
from the window, a winsome bird.

Only the moment exists, every moment
sliced thin and quick enough to hold no hope,

nor truth, no angle of light – only love. Only love,
You say. Only love, You say. Only love.

O child of God, exchange the emptiness
of hope for the fiery annihilation of Love.

Tickle and flinch

Ticklishness is a trust issue –
like flinching, though more benign.

We're all ticklish ... or worse,
when God puts His hands upon us –

spasmodic, spooked and shy. Trust must become
inherent and entrenched ... then, transcended.

Love transcends trust. Does away with it.
I've only had a crumb of that pie –

but, enough to know it tastes of annihilation.
The tongue is closer to the truth

(who would have thought?) when still,
than the ear or eye. The city of Paradise

lies beyond a great chasm. Its towers notch the sky.
Trust keeps us walking the rim of that chasm.

Love – annihilation –must somehow
give us wings to go the distance

between the gates of heaven
and the ground upon which we stand;

between God and His creatures, His children.
Only annihilation – when the game is over –

the great castle dissolved into nonexistence,
only annihilation (You say) bridges the gap.

O child of God, come to terms with your solitude.
The Beloved wants you all to Himself.

The Great Given

Until You entered the equation
God was ever the unknown Variable.

Upon Your silent vow, Impeccable Witness,
God now is the Great Given. The Great Given.

Has forever been the Great Given –
the Original, Irreducible Indivisible.

But, the problem remains – how to reach God.
Only when the evidence piles up around our ears

does non-existence become a possibility.
When the palette through the glass

is strained into one explosive point,
when delight becomes distraction,

insight – impediment; conclusions disallowed,
when every kiss is a sharp, bloody spur

and the analysis not worth the flesh
into which it is seared, then ...

the Great Given might appear
in the footlights to sort out

and reclaim a piece of Itself
among the scattered and lost debris.

O child of God, if the problem is insoluble ... why endure
this constant ache in your chest and head?

The silence of Your wine

My words fall upon deaf ears
so I tap them out; like an old movie,

more apparent in black and white.
Perhaps, following Your lead, I hope

for an intimacy through my fingers
unattainable through throat and tongue.

We are all tired of words, You say.
But words from You have become my comfort.

I'm ready, o Lord, to abandon
this conversation and communion

which sustains my faith and yet
increases my thirst; but, in their stead,

fill me up, o Lord, with the unchallenged,
unforced, unutterable silence of Your wine.

O child of God, there's no one to hear but God,
so you write poetry.

The great disrobing

Honor the sadra beneath the glass,
far from the flesh it touched,

the Reality, even farther;
beyond form and farther still ...

until you reach your own immortality.
Honor the sadra beneath the glass,

flesh hovering gently without
its safe, smooth surfaces

but, in the spirit, treat it roughly –
a stepping stone or, makeshift sail,

a knotted escape out the window,
a hastily wound turban in the noonday sun.

Taken from His body to aid in the great disrobing,
the nakedness it must all come down to,

a sadra should not only bend the knee
but break the heart and let the grace flow

from every deep and chambered encounter
with the One Who remains beyond ever

the reach of symbol, ritual, sanctification,
sentimentality and every palpable form.

O child of God, bow down to the holiness
within your own chest.

A poor man's truth

I would seal my lips. My pen put away,
my keyboard – abandon words ...

better still, opinions, queries, notions,
conjectures and suggestions

until I make the point
of every utterance ... praise. Praise!

Readily, would I praise –
unstintingly -- but, I am unable

to tell the Truth. And so I must resort
to a poor man's truth -- honesty,

broker the words faithfully
as I know how. These words

begin in the realm of praise,
begin in the realm of praise (!),

rasp and slice away, grind and whittle away
a measure of darkness, a measure of darkness,

a measure of darkness ...
tiny, slight but, steady on the mark,

flood the page and reward the heart with beauty,
with private confirmation and communion.

O child of God, abandon words
when they no longer connect.

The play of love

The angel gave Hafiz a choice –
beauty ... or, the source of beauty;

object of love ... or, its essence;
sensate flesh ... or, holy spirit.

An ordinary man – without thought –
reaches, innumerable lifetimes,

flesh for flesh, breath for breath,
for fragile beauty and rides that swell

of pleasure until it perishes beneath him.
The extraordinary man tries for both ...

and undermines himself – trying to swim the river,
pockets stuffed with gold.

A man of God (such as Hafiz)
gauges the price and is willing to pay;

chooses the source and the spirit –
sees through, sees through!

Forsakes the creation for the Creator –
a maiden for the Maker of maidens ...

and angels ... light and death, universes,
raptures, agony and the play of Love Itself.

O child of God, you know the rules of a game
you have not the courage to play.

Even your bones

By daily loss, the Way is gained,
the masters say, *loss upon loss ...*

until at last comes rest. Everything to God belongs ...
when you own nothing, disavow everything,

inside and out – from your endless, fleeting thoughts
to the mighty, roaring stars, the heart's collapse,

the soul's painful duties – nothing
for your shoulders to bear, even your bones

belong to Him and the clinging flesh, the fallen sparrow,
the numbered hairs, the firmament and the depths.

The world is won by those who let it go!
Let God grab it from your hands, heart

and head, strip you of the illusion of attachment
and limitation. Acquiesce, o lover, the masters say,

now ... where you are – in this fragmented life of fear.
Surrounded by God, come out – hands up and empty,

your heart an open palm, your head
a flowing stream laid at the Master's feet.

O child of God – *but, when you try and try*
the world is, then, beyond the winning.

Try to try

Two ways, You say, to love God –
own nothing, including yourself

or, live in the world, putting everyone else
ahead of you in the queue.

That lets me out – no way for me
to love God. Not this lifetime.

Eruch said, try to try. Try to try.
That's my this time lifetime – try to try, try to try.

Splendidly flawed, perfectly dear
near ones ecstatically drawing tears

from my world-weary eyes; try to try, try to try.
Sparks of pleasure, joy may animate me

now and then but nothing can rekindle
the fire in these sodden ashes.

Try to try, try to try. The thorn in the kiss –
ubiquitous Shiva – time like water,

washing away, washing away
the smooth, black slate, running through my fingers.

Try to try, try to try, eternal soul in mortal breast,
doubting everything but the dilemma

and You say the dilemma is illusion.
Try to try, try to try. To love God, try to try.

O child of God, your sword is made of fire.
Lay it at the feet of the Master.

Without expression

According to the Prayer,
God is without expression.

No wonder the God in You kept silent ...
while the fragrance of inner attainment

Your humanity expressed
in the world of forms –

truth, love, purity and beauty.
I circumambulate Your Samadhi,

o Qutub, studying every angle
to express a new perspective

or, reiterate, in a novel way, an old one,
my voluble moth-soul erratically mobile,

transitory, malleable, chimerical,
while You are fixed, silent, stalwart, eternal –

without expression, without expression –
expression requiring distance, need and duality.

O child of God, find the Oneness
that requires no communication.

Body language

Men's daily lives will be
the living precept (You promise).

The words I have not spoken
will come to life in them.

Meanwhile ... I study body languages
of myself and other lovers

of Your seven bodies, searching,
inside and out, for the birth of words

for years unspoken -- yet, shaped
a lifetime on earth, on earth,

o Emmanuel, Emmanuel.
Await the living, breathing words

among us, precepts sown by silence –
evidential change, redemption, salvation.

Your only miracle, You said –
to change the human heart.

Scholars scour the words you left behind.
I search for words You left unsaid,

in myself and others – to become the words,
to become the words You left unsaid.

O child of God, let it be, let it happen. Let it be,
leave it alone. Undisturbed ... undisturbed.

O shining city!

O Lord, my Lord, where and when shall union take place –
this homecoming for which my soul ceaselessly pines?

Spectral voices and music have entered my ears
from the crib and cradle, through the hard back pews,

on the Southern ether and the radio dials,
from behind the lecterns, choir lofts, baptismal pools –

o lovers, o sinners, it lies yonder, lies yonder –
across the river, through the gates of pearl,

the walls of jasper, above
the city foundations of twelve precious stones;

in a city – o shining city! – streets of gold,
among the clouds ... in the land of Beulah,

beyond the sun ... union lies, o pining hearts,
o tear-stained, heaving chests;

o lovers and sinners, lost and found, lost and found ...
wretched and redeemed, every head bowed, every eye closed,

knees bent and buckled, every heart broken.
O Beloved, I have heard Your promise my life long –

and others will hear it yet, pronounced above my grave –
and wonder, Lord, my Lord, where and when,

where and when, shall this union take place? Where
and when shall I enter, at last, the glorious gates of pearl?

O child of God, take comfort in the heart's evidence –
you are, indeed, a stranger in a strange land.

The ties that bind

The karmic dilemma
gathered and gleaned over the years –

in the fetal position,
roughly bound hands and feet,

drifting in and out of clarity
and when out of it –

chasing a sham of freedom everywhere
in this physical, sensual dream-like life.

Every Master worth His salt has pointed out –
even the slightest tug and accommodation

binds you all the more.
And so it comes down to

the unfettered tongue, the unobstructed throat.
O lovers, call His name –

the One whose nimble fingers
lovingly unsnarl, unwind.

Call Him to your side – the One whose mighty sword
the knotted tangles roots out and slices through.

Call His name! Lure Him with praise and song;
remembrance and repetition;

with your humility and your most
holy lying-down helplessness.

O child of God, the repetition of His name
(He promises) severs the ties that bind.

Sweet solace

... candles guttering, bottles empty,
the littered table abandoned;

bellies full; throats raspy with song –
one more, one more and still yet, one more –

companions reluctant to end the night.
Longing for God is the same fire

as solace found
in the impermanence of existence;

in the impermanence of self –
solace – sweet solace found

in the ethereal and illusory,
in abdication and surrender,

in the structure and promise,
the poetry and majesty of the game itself;

found by faith and grace – solace
by faith and grace, grace always there ...

always there – all there ever was
and all there ever will be.

O child of God, longing and solace are the same fire
taken from the One eternal, ever-abundant Source.

In the drink

Everyone is in the drink –
laboring to keep their heads above water;

no piece of solid real estate
in this vast sea of illusion

upon which to make a stand,
gain a foothold – a perspective, stability, bearings.

Some are swift and fancy swimmers,
others fat and lightly floating,

some sink like stones but,
everyone, everyone, is in the drink,

paddling about, waiting for the One
Who walks upon water;

Who surveys the horizon and sets the course;
Who offers navigation, buoyancy, consolation;

truth, hope, explanation.
Be kind, o child, and dubious,

studious and soft-spoken;
be clear-headed, one-pointed, alert.

O child of God, everyone is in the drink
until they drown in the Ocean of Love.

In lieu of silence

In lieu of silence, I offer this poem.
In lieu of surrender, I offer this prayer.

Unable with my whole heart to praise You,
I compose these poems of praise,

mitigated by inquiry and complaint;
by words themselves. In lieu of conviction,

I assiduously examine and guard my faith,
lest a wall should crumble, a foundation crack.

In my lack of poise,
I lay at Your feet my desperation

and because my obedience is so shaky,
I repeat constantly my repentances

for the breaking of my high-minded vows.
I can't live up to Your measure

but, You *are* the measure. It is You
for Whom I break my own silence,

reaching out of my shell with petitions,
questions, grievances and grief.

You are the Hub around which my thoughts,
my being revolve in this mad, whirling experience

in which I find myself and hope,
one day, to lose myself ... and find You.

O child of God, when a poem breaks your heart
you know you've moved a smidgen closer to the core.

The glue of faith

Surrender, my Beloved said.
Become all Mine when there is nothing

left of you. To surrender absolutely,
I surmised, absolute trust is required –

gathering the scattered shards
and splinters of my childhood trust

and, with the glue of faith, fashioning anew
that bright, sturdy vessel. When it had assumed

a fragile shadow of its former shape,
I brought it to the Lord for inspection.

In His infinite compassion, He stated –
You can't bring that through My door.

Your trust, He explained, *must also be surrendered.*
And I wandered into the desert,

my trust tucked loosely under my arm.
I can't let it go – it's my connection to Him.

I can't keep it – it's made of my own convictions.
Hold on to it, my Lord said. *Honor it. Drink from it.*

*Use it in your prayers ... until the day
you can successfully crush it under your heels.*

O child of God, illusion begets illusion.
Selfhood taints everything it touches.

Our life savings

God is love ... or else nothing matters.
Nothing matters, You say ... *but love*

for God. Love ... matters --
that it exists, that we have it to give.

Love is the knot at the end of our ropes;
the bookcase that swings open

to reveal a secret passageway;
the hidden compartment

where our life savings has been stashed.
Love is why everyone gets so excited

when they first come to You – like finding
banked coals aglow in the frozen tundra.

We don't listen, at first, about the near impossibility
of *becoming* that fire, about the hardships

of the long journey ahead – the burning part,
the dying part, the nothing-else-matters part,

so relieved are we to find that love exists,
that we can make love our God because He is.

O child of God, two measures of hope –
love exists and you have tasted a bit of it.

In the clenches

A half moon floats almost directly above,
silent in the blue morning sky –

you have to crane your neck to see it.
O my Angel, I'm left dim-witted, spent and sore –

I've been grappling with You
for ten thousand years(!) –

ceaselessly seeking explanations;
inexorably drawn to the Inexplicable.

The cross I'm nailed to – stretched in two directions –
is the intersection of the mortal and the divine.

When I entered the ring, someone took the stool –
there's no corner in which to rest

and in our brutal circling ... there's a loveless strategy
even in the clenches – biding my time,

gathering my strength and resistance,
fending off your unrelenting blows.

O child of God, dance earnestly around the ring,
dutifully engaged in the battle for your soul.

Ottoman

I consulted a dictionary,
thick as any gravestone,

the meaning of each word
only given in terms of other words

whose meanings must also be
looked up and so ...

around and around we go --
illusory, inclusive world of words

created by barking, braying,
warbling and lamenting,

cooing, crooning, flesh-throated human beings –
our wordiness letting no truth in edgewise.

Your love I find inexplicable, indefinable, unutterable –
Your love – all You ever talked about (in Your silence).

Silence I dare not keep – the truth of myself
might shine forth for all to see. I dare not shine.

I dare not embrace, so I go home
and write a poem about shining, embracing –

a pillow made of my dictionary,
an ottoman of my phonebook.

O child of God, words never tell the Truth
yet, they are the only means at your disposal.

Ocean planet

This is my prayer – forgive me, Lord,
for I cannot forgive myself.

My failures constant, my repentance
ever a step behind.

You say there's nothing to forgive but, from where
did this idea of perfection come

which mocks and haunts?
From a past before the sun woke up

and shone upon an ocean planet,
before the stars threw off their covers,

the moon sent spinning – when consciousness
went about urgently seeking to enter

the physical realm – poring over emerging mountains
and the cooling down stones?

A past of soul-perfection before the thick lens
of self began to distort the realm in two?

O child of God, return to perfection
by embracing your imperfect self.

O faith of mine

O faith of mine, o faith,
I run through you daily.

I run through you with feet of clay –
like running with a kite

over the hardscrabble landscape,
until the wind can catch it

and I can stop, stand my ground,
sufficient tension upon the string

to keep the kite aloft.
O faith of mine, o faith

of sticks and paper, string and wire,
I manage you warily, hands cupped in prayer.

You are my icon, my silent, bright relic.
You bind my life together at the end of this line –

my gathered, disparate, quavering self –
and keep my face turned upward

toward the floating, moon-like, bright-shining
kite above the hardscrabble turf.

O child of God, faith is the evidence of God's mercy –
the inward concern ... turned outward.

God was born

God was born (as any lover will attest)
at David Sassoon Hospital in Pune, India ...

more than a century ago now. That is to say,
God entered the mortal realm an embryo in a womb –

vulnerable, dependent, miniscule and yet, growing
inexorably toward fruition. Nothing can hold back God;

His precisely scheduled manifestation.
Even Jesus (of the ascension and the miraculous birth)

began a floating fish in a woman's belly.
O seeker of God ... God is within *you* ...

right *now* – (it's how He enters the realm).
Within you – vulnerable, dependent, miniscule, yes,

but growing every moment, inexorably toward fruition.
And, in the course of His love and law,

He shall outgrow the flesh that encapsulates Him,
transcend the mind that ensnares ... and escape

forever the narrow, bedimmed, illusory confines
of your self. O seeker, nothing can hold back

the God within you nor prevent His destined,
precisely scheduled manifestation.

O child of God, where is your patience? Everyone –
Meher Baba says –is destined for the supreme goal.

131

Over the jasper walls

If this was paradise, I would want out –
over the jasper walls one night ...

or ducking back through the pearly gates.
If pleasure reigned, every heart's desire

quelled and answered, suffering eased,
death overcome, I would still want to know –

to *know* -- not the truth but, Who. Who.
I believe, anyway. I feel as much.

If everyone on earth were angels of mercy --
wore wings -- of kindness, generosity,

I would still be missing a stone,
an aching hole in the wholeness. O Lord,

must my wanderings take me back ...
all the way ... all the way ... beyond, beyond?

Beyond, beyond ... is that home? That unimaginable,
perfect silence and stillness before the journey began;

before the imaginary bits of Yourself were gathered
and scattered and pressed into service?

Reaching down into myself, I yield, probe and open –
What is the essence of this longing and Who,

o Lord, o Lord – no names or descriptions –
Who is my Beloved? Who is my Beloved?

O child of God, let the tide of mystery within you
rise ... then, inexorably, sweep you away.

My baffled heart

The heart is a seed buried in the chest
due for an eventual flowering

or grit, perhaps, for a future pearl. Or, say,
the heart is a bird, its singing muted

by layers of flesh. I tell repeatedly my sons
I love them ... lest they forget ... lest they doubt;

lest they drift away, my throat bearing
a mere trembling resemblance to the truth

my baffled heart is unable to share.
You wore, o wordless One, Your heart

invariably on Your sleeve; Your love
Your presence, speechless and palpable,

awakened in Your *lovers'* chests; in their *own hearts*.
Such were the human changes You wrought.

Long after the husk and flesh were shed,
Your naked seed buried in that rocky soil,

Your presence, Your love awoke
in my stone tomb, my human, baffled heart –

Your love – wordless, eloquent, shared
across the chasm, through the lover's flesh,

lest I didn't know; lest I had forgotten; lest
I should ever doubt and become estranged.

O child of God, hold on to the silence
in which real things are given and received.

This riotous world

Headlong, fists-first, the young man
plunged into the world; got jostled

on busy thoroughfares, rubbed shoulders
in barrooms, sang from the backs

of hay wagons, on the tilted decks of ships–
searching for something he never found.

In the middle years, late-night,
he roamed, suburban avenues,

city alleyways, forest trails,
dry creek beds; sacred caves;

sat cross-legged on mountaintops;
wept into his bare hands.

Old now, the music of the world
seldom reaches him –

he rarely leaves the porch.
A voice counsels him to *turn in.*

Shut the world out.
Allow time to disengage.

O seeker, the voice says – *this entire existence,*
this tumbling, riotous world

has nothing to do with anything ...
except you and Him.   You and Him.

O child of God, you've been brought to a place
where escape is the only meaningful endeavor.

Sprawl and tangle

Imagine a path to the Path.
Not a path for a pilgrim to follow

but, a path which follows the pilgrim;
freely chosen yet, prior and post,

with strings attached, a web woven
in a realm obscure and deceptive,

every effort and action determined
by the soul's karmic sprawl and tangle.

Unable to choose wisely or freely
yet, unable to refrain from choosing,

inexorably wrought by the cast of a die
to live it, accept it, acquiesce

and yet, somehow, make it better,
holier, humbler, nearer to the goal.

Everything is necessary, my Beloved says,
until it is no longer necessary.

Everything, my Beloved says, is necessary
until it is ... necessary ... no ... longer.

O child of God, you are free, like Eruch, to choose
to become the slave of your Beloved.

Thread the needle

How many miles to Babylon? the children chant.
Three score and ten, comes the reply.

Can I get there by candle light?
Yes, and back again. And back again.

In time, Babylon, and imagination – half the distance
to heaven. Can I get there by candle light?

All there is to do in the game is laugh and run
and hold on tight – as the line weaves

and circles back ... and, one by one,
thread the needle, one by one.

How many miles to Babylon? Insurmountable
the distance, millenniums away and back again

yet, the game has wafted down as the children chant,
their queries if not replies resonating

in quickly-beating, childish hearts; run, laugh
and hold on tight. Lord, we want to know ...

how far and how we might arrive
at our destination and return home again.

All there is to do ... is to laugh and run, hold on tight.
Thread the needle, o child; thread the needle.

O child of God, play the game, hold on tight ...
though the journey seems uncharted and endless.

Just shining

You are the Light of the world
and light makes no sound. It just shines.

Those who couldn't see the Light asked for words.
You pointed out certain arrangements

resembling the Light and later wrung from the air
approximations that delighted Your lovers –

they printed up cards, pamphlets,
magazines and books. How sad for You,

at times, also, for the Mandali, Your flesh ablaze,
eyes aglow, the roaring fire inside

and Your lovers – in their blind faith –
praise and bow and plaintively beseech You

for descriptions of the Light. For evidence,
for instructions; for intimations,

for directions to the Light. O my Lord,
You are the Light of the world

and You took birth to shine Your Truth,
silently ... silent – just shining. Just shining.

O child of God, he who is blind, let him ...
muck about in the business of words.

The illusion of God's absence

The rich have their diamonds and pearls;
the poor – the moon and stars;

the pauper emerges from a cramped hovel,
peers upward into a starry night

going on forever. Upon every doorstep –
the infinite sky, the eternal now,

filling us up everywhere we turn
upon the spectrum of agony to ecstasy.

The Lord is our shepherd – we shall not want.
Every brimful moment – we shall not want.

No one is slighted; no one goes without.
Our inheritance – our just and proper due –

life in minutia, in all extremes,
the essence and price of being human.

Preference creates the illusion of want. Judgment
and desire create the illusion of God's absence.

O child of God, cultivate indiscriminate gratitude;
purchase Oneness with the jewel of desirelessness.

O child of God, in the stone's crevice
shall bloom the perfect rose.

Love interest

Existence You compare to a motion picture
with God playing every role.

You, of course, are the love interest.
When Your face hits the screen

every pulse quickens.
Let the storylines get too sad, predictable

and You are thrown into the mix,
to stir up the plot by espousing

the most difficult task in existence.
Love God, You say. Love God.

Again and again, You enter the picture
to round out and soften

God's rough edges, awaken
the human heart to love. To love.

You make it easy -- so that we might begin
our arduous approach to God;

to love God, to become God,
to become God the Beloved.

O child of God, impossible to love the self;
next to impossible to love the Self.

A drop of God's oil

Cover the earth with leather,
say the Buddhists, or shoe your feet.

But that bit of wisdom doesn't touch the pain
of our existential isolation.

A mile in my brother's shoes will show me
only the contours of the outer terrain –

nothing of the interior.
Loneliness is made of clay – our clay.

I can't be you; you can't be me
so we try to get to know one another.

How far apart! -- two people holding hands,
whispering into each other's ear.

Each human essence, the teachings say,
is a drop of God's oil.

Once the barrier is broken, the post
surrendered -- the oil blends, remaining

what it always was, always is –
unadulterated Oneness.

O child of God, try each moment to acknowledge
that drop of oil within you and everyone else.

The last resort

Most people come to You
(You have said) as a last resort.

There's a fundamental wounding
in coming to You, a violation of the self

in even our most timid of intimacies with God
or any of His manifestations.

In Your infinite mercy, You draw us past
our intuited fear and allow us our first

quavering steps toward annihilation,
gathering us in, tucking us under Your wing.

But, even after we become Your lovers,
years later, we often come to You

in pain and fear only when our most familiar
worldly comforts have been tried,

exhausted and found wanting,
our last resort yet ... because

within every surrender, every intimacy with God,
incrementally, now and then, here and there,

moment to moment, there is a fundamental
wounding, a violation of the self as we move

so timidly – a gesture, a word, a few steps,
an embrace – closer to our own annihilation.

O child of God, come unto the Ancient One,
the last resort, the final refuge of the soul.

The cabin in the woods

The windows are frosted over
and made of that primitive glass

that distorts every image but, through it,
shivering in the dark, I see a roaring fire,

a food-laden table, bottles of wine.
Why can't we go inside? I ask

the companion who brought me.
In due course, he answers. Once we enter,

he says, everything turns back to zero.
Everything will cease to exist ...

except that roaring fire which is,
at this moment, oblivious to itself.

We'll all go back ... to begin again.
The only way for that fire to be glimpsed,

to be desired and pursued,
captured and savored

is for it to first be viewed
from the outside looking in –

through these narrow, muddled,
distorting panes of glass.

O child of God, every moment has its value.
There is no place to get to.

And the Word was God

Small word – god. Like a grunt,
a groan breaking from our throats;

capitalized, modified by the pious –
Used profanely by sinners.

Forgive us, God, this small begrudged word
wedged into our vocabulary like an afterthought.

Words of worldliness – pleasure, flesh, riches,
savored by our mouths – luxury, lavish; sexuality,

sumptuousness, triumph, lasciviousness ....
O pilgrim, take god – that hard nugget of a word

and nurture it in your core
until it breaks you open,

breaks your world apart,
until a tree from its seed grows,

stretches, brushes, leaves and branches,
against the farthermost ends

of your thoughts, depths, faith,
experience and imagination.

O child of God, in the beginning was the Word ...
and the Word was God.

A nod and a wink

How ya doin'? I ask friends,
acquaintances, total strangers –

a form of greeting, no reply necessary.
No one knows the answer anyway.

Just the asking – throat to ear,
saying – we're all on the same ship,

surrounded and overwhelmed in our frailty,
our mortality, ignorance and ephemerality

by the Infinite, the Unpredictable and the Eternal.
We pass each other on the bridge

and ask, how ya' doin'?
The answer's always the same –

I'm alive. Surviving ... on the edge of terror
and catastrophe; skating

this depthless, unfathomable sea,
breathing moment to moment as freely as possible

in this inexplicable, fearsome
and wondrous existence of which

we have no real knowledge or conception.
We have only our faith ... and each other.

O child of God, how ya doin'?
Answer with a nod and a wink.

Room for God

Humility is hard to come by ...
(and I have so much to be humble about).

A toothless lion – pride; a gnawing rat.
Brave men have no pride;

even a humble man's courage
is not there when grasped;

a humble man – he's no hero ... nor saint.
Humility and its poverty

leave room for nothing else
except, maybe, God

to enter when the walls are rubble,
where a man stands

naked and armless, without pride or courage.
Then, maybe, there's room for God.

O child of God, Meher's love, so freely given,
apparently, demands every last thing in return.

My prayer-cupped hands

Muslim men in the East, I'm told,
smoke biddies channeled

through cupped hands –
Mohammed having forbid tobacco

to ever touch their lips.
This is the kind of love song

with which I nightly serenade my Beloved,
exploring the convoluted ways

I might obey my Lord
and savor the smoke at the same time.

It is the illusion of our maneuverability
that keeps paradise just out of grasp.

Until I become that fabled ant
beneath the elephant's foot,

my cleverness and desire will ever reach out
for the birds in the bush and let loose

the one captured and singing
in my prayer-cupped hands.

O child of God, obey your Beloved and refrain
from the lies you tell yourself daily.

Truth be told

Truth be told, my Master was silent.
Truth be told, silence was the essence

of His message. O, He promised
on numerous occasions to speak

the Word of words ... some forty-odd years ...
but nary a word He left us – no goodbye,

no parting wisdom, trading one silence for another.
Such is our dilemma, o lovers, in telling others

of His silence and His broken promises,
of our fascination with the One

Who refused to be glib, pedantic,
predictable in the Truth; Who spoke

somehow beyond throat and ear, beyond
forced and roughly shaped sounds.

I suggest we must, in the end,
resort to our own brand of silence

and pray Truth be told, His Truth –
in all its palpable, wordless splendor –

be told, be told, be told within each
God-conscripted, fatefully chosen breast.

O child of God, your job is to love Him.
His job is ... everything else.

Dream house

Each morning I build my dream house
on a narrow spit in the great blue sea,

a citadel rising and shining
along the length of the day.

Each night, the tide turns, invades the shore –
everything uprooted, pulled asunder

by the flooding waters. I observe the ruination
and, with canny clarity, the prejudice

and error, the insularity and pride with which
I had stood sure-footed by light of day.

Curled up and trembling in the dark,
from my heart's incontestable bottom,

I call Your name until a light breaks over the horizon –
Your presence, a bulwark against the blows

of the overwhelming sea.
I arise, on Your assurances,

for another morning prayer, another
whole-hearted, arduous day of labor

upon the house of my dreams,
upon that narrow spit in the great blue sea.

O child of God, doubt yourself and trust Meher.
Dissolution is opportunity; obliteration – absolution.

Foreign shore

The dot of an umbrella thwarting
the mighty sun and the rain – imagine that!

The ball of an eye
containing mountains.

God (You say) is the Ocean of Love.
Why on earth then, is Love such a rarity?

If it shines everywhere, falls like rain
and I don't know enough to strip down

and run around in it, why then
is there such a longing in my soul?

One cup of wine – I get weepy, incoherent.
Imagine an Ocean of It!

I'm too small to drown, too lightweight,
too hard-shelled to soak It up

and sink to the bottom. Grimly, I clutch
that bit of debris known as other-than-Ocean,

floating, ever floating, upon the surface
of my obliteration and liberation,

tossed up again and again
onto the wild, foreign shore.

Otherness is illusion, Meher said.
You and I are not we, but One.

O child of God, otherness is illusion.
You and the Ocean are not two, but One.

The cleft of flesh

It shone through, Mani said.
It shone through. Your divinity.

Particularly as the coat frayed;
split-seamed and threadbare.

Your lovers clamored those latter days
for the nectar of Your presence –

It shone through. And nowadays
in a random soul, coat perforated

by the casual sorrows of human existence,
the loneliness and the long night-vigils,

whose faith and the thread of Your Light
have kept stitched together,

It shines through. Shines through.
With God's Light behind every star

and space a threadbare cloak,
so through the cleft of flesh

the Light pours into this dusky realm.
Cleft, o lovers, for thee and me.

O child of God. There was a glow,
said Mani. There was a definite glow.

Crowded house

You often slip my mind
but are lodged ever firmly in my chest –

the best part of me now. The real part.
Neglected at times in the crowded house –

guests milling about, unintended, uninvited.
Luminous in Your flowing white gown,

I inch toward You, working the crowd,
strangers tugging at my sleeve,

inserting themselves between us,
spinning me around by the shoulder.

Everyone has something important to tell me.
I reach You and fall at Your feet.

When I lift my head the house is empty
save for You and me. I keep all sorts

of images like this in my head.
But, I want to know You in my chest –

aglow in the iron-ribbed furnace,
cheeks ruddy, neck flushed,

eyes green fire, tears unbidden.
I want You to leave me impaired –

sated, wondrous and bewildered,
mouth clamped shut so no smoke escapes.

O child of God, oneness begins with constancy
so complete it shatters the illusion of duality.

Due inheritance

Soon after birth, she was left beside a bridge.
They had not the heart like so many others

to throw her into the river. It's easy now –
and then – to trace the royalty of her blood,

the inherent beauty, the glow of her holiness.
In fact, it's evident in all their faces –

everyone born into this realm is abandoned at birth.
Who, then, dares implant such a longing –

that each child should expect sheltering
and nourishment, indulgence and praise?

O fellow children of God, heirs to the kingdom,
when shall we accept the mantle of our nobility?

When shall we demand
with trembling voice and shaking fist

our due inheritance – and nothing less?
The heart will hold its tongue

for millenniums, submissive to the senses,
to circumstances, ignorance and death,

but it knows, it knows, it *knows* ...
and once it begins to unfold, to strengthen and rise,

our demeanor and likeness to the King become
ever more transparent, self-evident and undeniable.

O children of God, assume the kingdom's throne
by becoming who you already are.

Chanji

He found you in Chowpatty
washed up on the beach

by life's betrayals, cruel vicissitudes.
You were ready to drown by then,

not caring if you lived or died.
He persuaded you

to go a-travelin' with Him.
Apparently, the Way is so narrow

there's only room for one
to walk it at a time

which doesn't mean
we go it alone

but, that we must become one
with our traveling companion.

Chanji, by the end of his days,
was one with You, ready for drowning,

not caring if he lived or died
as long as it pleased his Master.

O child of God, nothing ever changes ... it just gets larger –
more height, breadth and depth than we could ever imagine.

Love unbidden

Long after You'd dropped the body,
her wish granted – You appearing in the flesh.

Crushed and weeping, she told Eruch –
I should have asked for love.

I should have asked for love.
Looking back down

the bone-littered path,
a hundred-eighty degree swing

to the narrow cleft
in the fog-shrouded hills,

under the heft of my pack, my heart
resigned to dying almost certainly

with one more inescapable regret –
those days, while I had the chance,

running through my fingers
and all the earthly desires, instead ...

I should have asked for love.
I should have asked for love.

O child of God, each moment you are being given
love unrecognized and unbidden.

The secret

I go around with a crushing desire
to talk about that which I do not know.

Something to do with a Lion
Who devours Its lover.

Love – the big cat
Who stole my Lord's tongue,

swallowed up Merwan
and began a silent prowling.

Love is a secret, my Lord said, to be kept.
All I'm saying, Lord –

let me in on the secret.
Let me keep it *with* You.

Let me keep it *with* You forever
until forever is no more.

O child of God, prove trustworthy;
He'll whisper it in your ear.

Precious cargo

Read it until it sings in your veins!
You said of God Speaks.

All remembrance should be like that –
vascular, in the marrow; a deep

and irresistible recognition; a light
dispelling the shadows

in which incredulity and indifference breed,
reestablishing our ancient-most

connection with reality;
... until it sings in your veins!

On the practical side, it should be sturdy
and lightweight, wieldy – a convenient apparatus

for exposing and relinquishing
the temporal and the illusory;

unable to grasp our intended
distractions and indulgences,

finding our hands (heads, throats)
ever full and otherwise occupied

by a pure and most precious cargo –
Your name, Your image, Your presence.

O child of God, *Remember Me* is a *question*.
Search your innermost depths to find the answer.

Imaginary wristwatch

I haven't much time, You gesture,
(turned up at my door for a visit)

wagging a finger, tapping
an imaginary wristwatch. *Stay present,*

You say. *Fearlessly value each moment.*
But, serving tea, I begin to worry –

my china set cheap and tarnished;
my tea of low quality; fingers trembling,

words awkward. I get shaky
whenever You look my way.

I worry some imprudent word or gesture
might send You prematurely to the door.

Which prompts a vision of my house
even bleaker than before

with You gone from it.
After a time, You rise;

take Your leave. *Next time,*
You gesture, *next time,*

(tapping the imaginary wristwatch) –
trust Me with your life!

O child of God, how foolish! Afraid
of losing that which is eternally present.

It was love

I'd painted myself into a corner –
I felt pure there and wise;

one hand tied behind my back;
watching the paint dry; no room

for a wrong move, the only unfinished part
now tucked firmly under my prayer mat.

Reverently, I pledged my life to You.
This is your life? You asked.

A corner where two walls meet?
It was love that lured me into the sunlight,

lifted me from the mat, escaping
precariously through an open window.

Love that enlivened me, made me more
(for better or worse) human.

Love God-sent, threaded through a heart
human like mine, but fearless, roaring like a lion.

Hold My hand, You said.
I'll give you a tour of My creation.

O child of God, offer no gesture
cheapened by fear and accommodation.

Loose talk

I drift through the loose talk ...
of liberation, realization,

seven planes, the imminent
golden age of the new humanity.

Eternally benevolent, (the prayer goes)
God is. Eternity's a long time.

Surely His benevolence
gets stretched mighty thin.

Cresting the hill, I view the next
lonely stretch of highway.

Whoever makes it
to those distant mountains

won't be me. I don't know who
he will be but I wish him well.

It takes a blind, penetrating sorrow
to hope for more – in the long view –

from our Creator than His ultimate,
unconcerned benevolence; the Creator

of this intricate, unfathomable,
ever-unfolding, tear-and-blood-soaked game.

O child of God, a glint in the current's flow;
a spark from the blacksmith's hammer.

Our friendship

February 10, 1954 – You declared Yourself
Avatar of the Age! That's nice.

A more important event for me –
(I'm not sure of the date) –

You declared Yourself my friend.
Sorry, to be so self-fixated, so non-global.

You got through to me.
While I was keeping to myself.

Reached out and took
a clenched and diffident hand.

Since then, my every transmutation
has been shaped, guided

and colored by Your presence.
I was keeping my distance

(it was all I knew to do).
You got through to me –

lobbying intently, kindly insistent.
Lord, let my gratitude and our friendship

become one day a path
to Your love ... and to my surrender.

O child of God, Meher got through to you
by coming from the inside out!

Waiting in the wings

The moon is a disc, not a sphere.
Flat as the earth; the sea

pasted onto the bottom of the sky;
stars poking through a threadbare canvas.

I've turned away from the latest backdrop,
heading toward the interior.

It's all to be pulled down anyway
at the performance's end.

We flow through time apparently
but, also, time flows through us,

life delivered daily to our door.
How could I ever cease to exist?

If I cease, existence ceases, the void
once more reigns and even then ...

I'll be waiting in the wings.
The scenery incessantly changes but, still

I stride the stage, emoting, aggrandizing,
gesticulating, playing it to the hilt.

O child of God, follow the script.
The pageant is endless; without resolution.

Birds made of sky

... slice effortlessly through the ether –
no cleaving upon their approach,

no melding in their wake,
surrounded by silence thoroughly,

no residue nor resistance, birds made of sky.
To surrender must be to move

through existence like that – plowing through
time's flow and yet, somehow, adrift upon it;

no mechanics of survival; coming
from nowhere; being taken no place.

I spruce up surrender in my timidity –
display it in the most flattering light.

Human beings need that – ever measuring,
thinking in terms of loss and gain,

getting from here to there, but surrender,
apparently, must be undertaken

for its own sake; for truth's sake,
whatever the cost or outcome

because it *is* truth, the only truth
when nothing else but the truth will do.

O child of God, enter the flow of time
to escape the flow of time.

Elegy

Not a word of scripture to be quoted
over these bones but, at graveside,

he would have tolerated a short, silent prayer.
He took it as it came; for what it was worth.

Good for the sake of righteousness.
Honest in the cause of truth.

Brave for honor's sake.
Kind by decree of the human heart.

He'd put aside any fanciful notions
of heavenly reward or his possible rebirth –

(he was convinced of his own annihilation)
and thus, resolutely, he went to his death.

Quietly cherishing joy, enduring the pain,
he came closer to surrender

than any religious man I know. If he lacked anything,
it was the imagination and longing to be anything

other than the man he was.
As they lower his body now into the grave

I am struck by how closely
a coffin resembles a crib.

O child of God, to surrender is to yield,
earnestly and humbly, to your destiny.

The water of Jesus

Hope springs eternal, Pope observed.
A blessing, a heavenly confirmation.

But, one day, the teachings suggest,
we shall grow weary of it.

Faintly odious it'll become,
oily, brackish on the tongue,

and lose its allure, just another meaningless
babble for our ears to endure.

We'll see it as a substitute,
a tainted approximation of the *Living Water.*

One day its grip shall loosen; we'll let it slip
downstream through our prayer-cupped hands.

We'll lose our way, one day, to that well,
so that we might find another, taking freely

the water of Jesus, springing up also
in the human breast – of life everlasting.

We'll partake of that water, o seekers,
and never thirst again.

O child of God, whosoever will, let him come
and take freely the Water of Life.

An effortless endeavor

Seekers of God were drawn to You early on,
prepared to overcome every obstacle to liberation.

They begged You to instruct them in the Way;
to speak into their ears the Word of words.

You entered the Jhopdi one evening;
emerged wordless for the rest of Your life.

Your fingers spoke – at everyone's insistence –
of love, obedience and surrender.

Love – not the least bit amenable to force or will.
Obedience – mere disciplined ambition

unless prompted by a guileless heart.
Surrender – a letting go, a giving up

of all hope and desires, low and high.
Love, obedience, surrender –

each an effortless endeavor,
dependent upon the Master's grace.

Eruch proposed determination –
not quite effort – but, something to do

while waiting for the buds to unlimber, the fruit to soften,
the wine to ferment in its ancient wooden casks.

O child of God, embrace the process.
It is *that* to which we must surrender.

The bell is struck

The butterfly delicately (at times, awkwardly)
extricates itself from the cocoon,

repeating constantly the Prayer of Repentance,
bidding its old form, old self goodbye.

The Prayer says – the bell is struck,
(the fight is over) the hammer unhanded.

Its reverberations will empty themselves
and recede irrevocably into the silence.

The Prayer is of clinging, half-forgotten
dreams of the old life, the old form

as the soul awakens from its aeons-deep slumber.
Repentance is always backward-looking.

The Prayer should be spoken face-forward,
midstride, tossed earnestly over the shoulder,

discarded and forgotten as we tramp
the new stretch of highway beneath our feet.

O child of God, the Prayer is a reminder
of who you were before the Awakener struck!

Furrow the field

Only what is heavy has value, Kundera wrote,
(speaking of compassion).

We're merely floating, without it –
disengaged ciphers, shirkers, lightweights.

The world is a dream, so says my Lord,
without substance or weight, one big zero

yet, we are instructed to labor mightily,
shoulder to the plow,

turn the other cheek, offering our coats as well as shirts.
Who will supply the wings to float us

above the grief and suffering?
I will give you rest, Jesus said. *My burden is light.*

The Christ comes (according to the scriptures)
not to lift our burdens but to show us how

to disperse the fear and pain,
to shrug our shoulders, drop the reins,

letting the team and the plow bear the weight
and furrow the field, pulling their own intrinsic way.

O child of God, let the yoke of the Christ reveal
the insubstantiality of this sad, illusory world.

The evergreen shore

When the ice got thin, I stretched out flat –
distributing my weight, panicked and motionless,

so I was prostrate when You appeared,
a bright flame on the opposite bank.

I began to hope –
though You'd lobbied against it.

I began to learn –
though You'd not come for that.

I began to trust –
though You discouraged complacency.

I began to awaken –
though You remained silent as a Tomb.

After much spent patience,
subtle doting and cajoling,

I began sliding along on my belly
and lately, the arduous climb

to my feet, the risking of everything
to get nearer to You,

that beckoning flame
on the evergreen shore.

O child of God, Peter walked on *water*
with Jesus there to strengthen his faith.

The tomb of the now

Shake the shadowing past, o lover;
leap ... at the last possible moment –

(every possible moment) –
from the departing train.

Ditch that tiresome chaperone,
cynical governor and guide.

You'll end up, likely, on the wrong side
of the tracks. Learn your way around.

Reject the pitches of the barkers and carnies –
the winking future, the lurid rarees;

slip out of the rickety constructs
of the row houses and seaside pavilions.

Enter the tomb of the now.
Leave your strategies, tendril desires

and neurosis with your sandals –
outside that holy sepulcher. (The teachings say)

rest there – while you still have a body;
find space ... enough to accede and receive;

find death with all its accompanying peace
in the happy, carefree tomb of the now.

O child of God, pare down nearer and nearer
to the only one holy, eternal, unfolding moment.

What God is not

We're to become dust, says my Lord.
What value has dust? Next to nothing.

Tramped on, kicked around, beaten down –
lowly and compliant as a sandal print.

Jesus became dust –
stripped and spat upon,

mocked and rejected,
a carcass hanging from a nail,

far from God's glory as a man could get.
To unite with God, apparently,

we must choose to become exactly
what God is not – a mote of dust –

(the perfect counterweight);
dust – because God is immaculate;

because He is majestic, singular;
because God is dynamic, creative, alive!

To unite, o seeker, with the living
God Eternal, we must choose to die

beyond any hope
of resurrection or salvation.

O child of God, from your dust-clotted throat
sing now, sing – we are not we but one.

O wayfarer

You ordered aristocratic Norina,
much to her humiliation,

to return, again and again,
to the ship's Captain posing

the same question each time –
when shall we arrive?

Courteous, at first, annoyed and then irate,
he banned her, at last, from the bridge,

judging the Princess to have, somewhere
along the voyage, lost her mind.

A lesson in humble submission for Norina –
(and for every lover thereafter)

but, also, something more ... sinking deeper
into our bones and blood – and it's this –

the Captain commands the ship ...
plots the course, schedules the arrival,

knows precisely when and how
the destination should be reached.

Absurdity, sheer lunacy are our fears, inquiries,
gestures, inputs, urgencies and desires.

Lay back, o wayfarer. Embrace and endure in silence,
the remainder of your lonely voyage home.

O child of God, so many lessons from the One
Who did not come to teach.

The death of self

I need to get a grip.
Blood has slickened the shaft

of the arrow sticking from my chest.
It's love that bloodies the water,

seeping through from another realm;
sets things spinning; tainted,

myopic, half a bubble out of plumb.
If I could see clearly where myself ends

and others begin, I could count my charges,
leave others to their own tallies.

Love turns virtue into an impediment,
piety into predicament; divinity is in the blood,

the humble cloaks of our beings
shot through with silver and gold.

It's love that hobbles and wounds;
the taste of blood creates such a *hunger* –

such a *longing* to be devoured (forever) –
heart, soul, blood and bones.

O child of God, love is the rasp and the balm
which hastens the death of self.

Endless highway

A breach has developed
between myself and life –

immeasurably subtle yet,
discernible ... discernible.

I keep coming back to it
or, it keeps coming back to me,

a tear in the fabric; a peering through –
deeper, essential, within me and yet, also ...

flowing towards me –
a hint of my immortality –

to match existence, to match God.
I strongly suspect then

this flowing towards me continuously
has been flowing towards me eternally.

I turn another corner and know,
or suspect I know, there'll always be

another corner to turn, always ...
this being just another inimitable

stretch on an endless highway
to nowhere, forever and ever ... without end, amen.

O child of God, what destination lies beyond infinity?
On what date shall your eternity come to an end?

Whimsy

A bit of whimsy, says my Lord –
God's idle curiosity – striking up Creation,

freshly awakened, wondering, *Who am I?*
No whimsy, apparently since, however,

in this inevitable, sequential unfolding of existence
according to the inviolate laws of fate.

This is not a game of chance
(or whimsy) in which we are engaged,

not a contest or competition, this living creation
which is also an ongoing discovery;

this relentless interrogation
and its unraveling answer,

this in no game of chance.
Through alternate phases of sorrow, joy,

pleasure, pain, life and death we hurtle
at the ultimate mercy of the only One

in existence sovereign and almighty enough
to indulge in a bit of whimsy.

O child of God, surrender to the Inevitable.
No pause, no pardon, no rest, no turning back now.

The human chapters

Rings true on paper – but, by the book,
characters tend to leap off the page

as we thumb the human chapters –
leaves of crushed bones, tautly stretched skin,

blood-red ink. Virtue, fidelity strained out of proportion,
never again to assume their original shape.

Leave all, said my Beloved, and follow Me.
Our one true Friend but,

that does not absolve us of our infidelities.
Maybe, each is destined to wear the robe of Abraham.

The best I could muster now would be to hand God
the knife, curl up beside my son on the offering stone.

Unfit, unripe by my infidelity but, surely,
not abandoned by my one true Friend.

Thin scriptures, gold-trimmed, rattle the pages;
columned, annotated truths ring hollow

when blood spills, bones get broken;
when loved ones, weeping, appear

among those left behind. Then, words of truth prove
not worth the paper upon which they are written.

O child of God, beware of truth small enough
to fit into discourse and sutras, parable and song.

Salt flat

Existence, said my Lord, is a big fat zero.
Buddhists say the same – trying to shoo

everyone through the narrow slit of a door
beyond which lies, not paradise, but a vast,

flat, uninhabitable terrain.
Surrender, it would seem, amounts

to encountering every (blessed) moment
as the wondrous insignificance that It is –

life becomes death, soul becomes Soul,
illusion becomes Truth, zero becomes Everything.

And we, o pilgrims, become God,
gliding through, gliding through –

in the fine release, the swift transparency,
the invulnerable poise of every (blessed) moment.

Not a narrow path to follow,
nor a mountain to scale in the distance

but, an endless salt flat, in every direction equal,
to espy, acknowledge and wander

until we make our worthy return
to the Ocean from which we came.

O child of God, to surrender is to stop trying
to make something out of nothing.

In the hothouse

Fated the nightingale, the faithless rose
to forsake for the Maker of roses.

Such a leap comes about
only in timid, painful increments

here and there of mud-caked creatures.
The draw of bodies, the comely flesh

alter over time to the allure of human courage,
innate goodness, virtue and fidelity.

Clay to clay, we play with fire,
explore our capacities, pay the price

for the glamour, extravagant promises
of our budding, adulterated love

until love becomes purely the only tie that binds.
Then come, o Lord of Love, to wield Your axe!

O child of God, in the hothouse of human love
the heart tends and refines the timorous rose.

Water strider

Whatever you say about God,
declared Meister Eckhart, *is untrue.*

(Including, presumably, his own
aforementioned pronouncement).

Buddha simply smiled and upheld a flower.
Meher stopped speaking altogether.

It was the best He could do for His lovers –
with their scaled eyes, human ears

and brains; fledgling hearts
beating erratically in their chests.

This poetry is not about God
but about the swirling images

and ideas surrounding God.
The water strider knows well its milieu

but it cannot, could never (spindly lightweight),
fathom the depths below the surface;

incapable of deep submersion;
incapable of ever drowning.

O child of God, Meher gives you words
in lieu of the real things.

Of resolution and resurrection

Beauty becomes a quiet comfort
in the latter years, giving of its depth

and essence without intentions or purpose,
earning our honor and attention

by virtue of its mere existence.
One day Truth will be like that.

We'll cling to it even through
the most bitter of circumstances,

the most fearsome grief ... because it lies
so purely, so resolutely beyond our grasp.

It will taste medicinal by then –
of resolution and resurrection.

One day Truth will come to our door
so pure, so vulnerable, so lovely

it will be beyond us
to ever deny it anything.

O child of God, pray for the day truth, love and beauty
all are expressed by the same silent word.

Here is the crush

Here is the crush,
garnered and pressed;

a hitch in the stream,
a knot in the grain,

an opacity in the clear, flat glass.
Purity is imperceptible.

Light must be fractured
(and there is a certain violence to it)

to yield its colors. Here is the eternal,
indiscernible stillness

cropped, pared, hewn, here and there,
moment to moment, into illusory pieces.

Here is the inaudible essence
below the accompanying wail

and whine of the spinning orbs.
Here is the spangled sky, the lurch and yaw.

Here is the price God must pay
to perceive Himself.

O child of God, it's something about
looking through a glass darkly.

Inarticulate Truth

Love, You've come and gone,
the mystery ever deepening;

dropped in, kissed and hovered,
glided, flitted like an angel;

buried like a treasure,
an intractable seed in the stony soil.

Countless discourses, teaching stories,
elucidations and admonitions

and we're no deeper satisfactorily
into the mystery than before,

Your tangible, sensual advent
fading now into myth and history,

into the culling of the gist
and the choosing up of sides.

After a lifetime of frank,
genuine, animate Example,

the mystery has only deepened.
We're no nearer (it seems) to hearing

or bearing the inarticulate Truth
of Who You really are.

O child of God, Meher Baba best
explained Himself in eloquent, holy silence.

Of the eternal

The Gita says, what is born must die.
And as the bodies pile up,

our noses continually rubbed in the dust,
we begin to tremble before such a truth.

Yet, we are made also of the eternal
and therein a subtle assurance lies –

what is born must die –
the temporal self, born of ignorance,

vainly asserting its sovereignty
through numberless lifetimes and deaths –

by the same stark truth
must someday die ... eternally

while the God part of us,
the part *never* born ...

can never die.
Can never die.

O child of God, take note of death
only as a harbinger of life eternal.

This marvelous deception

Each moment of this realm drenched
in sweet, sorrowful parting;

this tangled web (You say) woven
by our own inherent duplicity.

I know what I need to do (according to You).
I haven't the courage, faith or desire.

I opt for the occasional and inevitable
sting of serving two masters,

savoring the free range between houses,
the seductive illusion beyond each gate –

the illusion of not being a slave.
There exists an intoxicating glamour

where flesh meets dust;
where flesh meets dust,

though tainted and tinged with sorrow,
we panic, grasp and cling,

in the impetuous moment, seemingly,
to the only chance we might ever have for heaven.

O child of God, weep for this marvelous deception.
Here is the place for tears.

The simple of heart

As a child, like a bird in a cage,
everywhere I went, I took Jesus

and the song of Jesus with me
but, the world easily crushed

and scattered that cage;
the bird flew and the song I heard no more.

Until Your song.
Like a bird in a cage,

I take You everywhere.
Now *that* cage is coming apart

not from the crush of the world
but, from the inside out,

the bird and its song too deep,
too large, too strong, too universal

for the cage to hold.
What once had meaning,

now has three meanings,
a thousand meanings,

multifarious, ever-shifting
and the whispering love song within

echoes from the bars and rafters
of this realm's farthest reaches.

O child of God, His song is for the simple of heart.
Take it with you everywhere you go.

Our cloven hearts

A fire in the joy; a fire in the grief;
a fire in the salt of our tears,

the chafe of our fetters;
a flame at the end

of our ever-shortening fuse –
there's a burning every moment,

our blood pushed and pressured
through its circuitous, destined path.

To seek within, the longing for God,
moving through our each

unique and curious lives,
the inner urgency and a goad

to turn us from the dream,
we need only dip our torches

into the ever-present, ever-burning
flame of our error, in the caldron

of our cloven hearts, the ubiquitous,
ever-present fire of our exile.

O child of God, longing for God is the blood-deep
remembrance of an ancient and abandoned placidity.

Your good graces

Lord, accept me as a gift.
I'm all wrapped up in myself;

the measure of everything
and still the world doesn't fit.

I should stop thinking of myself;
I should stop thinking of You

and how to worm my way
into Your good graces;

abandon efforts to gain
advantage and win the prize;

fall back on my groping, inchoate heart.
Be who I am. What a concept!

Ignorant, vulnerable, mute and motionless,
weathered down to the bone.

O, but spiritual poise like that,
surrender like *that*,

faith of *that* measure
comes at the heavy price

of all my intrinsic props and illusions –
my presumed mobility, autonomy, merit and clout.

O child of God, Meher said, "*Want what I want.*"
But, o pilgrim, ... the Godman wants nothing.

In the wake of Your silence

Your image in the neem tree
outside Mehera's window,

sort of a toss-away miracle –
like a chip falling where it may –

a goodbye kiss after dropping
Your coat – obvious, irrefutable.

Not so obvious, irrefutable always –
Your handiwork, patterns You left

in the wake of Your silence
and non-teaching

about how the game works,
how it should be played;

about Your constant companionship.
Not so certain, evident as the tree

but, there for the ear, eye, heart and brain
to imagine, to accept, more or less on faith,

here and there, Your mark
as a signpost, a milestone, a roadblock;

as a prodding, sweet succor, a timely cue;
as a kiss – Your silent, intimate assurance.

O child of God, not a sparrow falls
contrary to His plan and will.

God in heaven

I come to You because there's no one else.
Others who would comfort me, help me,

who love me, would only be, in their flesh,
further burdened by my grief.

There's no one else.
Whether the pressures subside or deepen,

(You say) You are to blame
and viewing this blighted realm's

daily mayhem, horrific circumstances –
all of which happen on Your watch –

if I had another throat in which to bury my face,
another chest to soak with tears,

(You know) I would hurry to it.
Embrace a different hope.

Yet, again, God in heaven, I turn to You,
on hands and knees calling Your name,

my heart laid bare; I ask –
am I not Your child?

O child of God, whatever God's love for you,
He's the only hope you have.

His perfect humanity

To walk the earth ... God becomes Godman.
This makes perfect sense –

the One, entering the realm of duality
must split Himself in two

in order to be seen and heard.
God alone is too terrible to approach

with our paltry hearts and hands
but, the Godman we can embrace,

praise His perfect humanity, His purity and virtue
and blame God (in the backs of our minds)

for the atrocities and injustices
which occur daily in this dual existence.

God lures us away from ourselves ... toward Him
with the Love-personified,

perfectly human Godman
with Whom we may easily identify

until we surrender the last of our veils
and barriers and turn our human faces

toward the terrible Truth
of Who He really is.

O child of God, who are *you*?
God alone exists.

The giver-away

Somewhere down the road
you met your Master

perhaps, millenniums ago,
the start of an arduous and tedious process –

the transfer of ownership. Or, maybe,
you were just nine years old –

giving Jesus your trembling life
aware not of how deeply thorough

your surrender must be,
as you know not now what you might do

to reach that critical depth
but, beginning to see

your well-connected, in-the-flesh self –
its deeply-rooted loves, alliances,

duties and responsibilities –
(to your utter shock) has no skin in the game.

Give your life to Jesus because,
(they should have told you)

at any moment, the chit may be
called in for payment due.

Surrender (your life) to the ultimate admission
that owning nothing, you do not exist.

O child of God, love (somehow) is the ultimate destroyer,
the giver-away of everything you think you own.

The rumor of love

Seeker of God, you call yourself
but, in truth, all you've ever sought –

(chased your whole life long) – is the faint,
elusive, barely audible rumor of love.

(What a lonely life you've led!)
You have loved as much as most,

yet, (even so) it seemed always
more a suggestion, a penciled-in sketch.

What need would you have for God
if a deep, massive, substantive love

came swelling in? Love enough to drown in;
not just the heart but the soul, too ... carried away;

drown the universe
farther than the eye can see,

the mind can imagine,
the heart can hold out for.

It breaks with longing so desperately, your heart
(according to the scriptures) for wholeness lost –

the rejoining of your detached self
to the Source of Truth. O seeker!

The rumor you chase starts with the moan
and murmur of your own incontiguous heart.

O child of God, the seeker is the Sought,
Meher says. God is love.

The beauty and necessity

At first, to move away from the world
is to move toward God but, make no mistake,

at some point, to move away from anything
is to move away from God.

This is not a decision to make
but, a beginning to see

the beauty and necessity of every moment.
Nothing happens twice but, patterns recur –

not to learn the lesson (at last)
but, to drain it dry,

dipping the ladle deeper and deeper
or, maybe it never gets empty

because the Essence is there
every moment, every ladleful,

when we reach a point of seeing deeply enough,
seeing all the way through to the other side.

O child of God, twist and turn or, concede and release,
God has you irrevocably in His net.

Not this

Neti, neti goes the Gita;
not this, not this.

Try it after each phrase
in the Prayer of Repentance,

neti, neti – not what I expected, Lord –
not this; not what I meant to say;

it wasn't what I lacked after all;
it blew up in my face, Lord;

neti, neti – not what I'd hoped for;
insufficient, unsatisfactory;

lost now – slipped away;
not this, not this, Lord, not this –

not what I wanted;
not what's in my heart;

not at all what I'd envisioned.
Neti, neti; neti, neti –

the clock is ticking away
the moments of choice, attachment and hope;

the constant failures we speak of –
being fooled again and again

by illusions self-created
through our ignorance and limitations.

O child of God, to repent of our failures is to list
the illusions we fall for moment to moment.

A babe in the woods

I fell for the world
and all its promises,

dream remnants
strewn and discarded

over a sad and painful terrain
and now I have fallen for You.

Will You let me down?
A babe in the woods

to be led to and fro,
hither and yon,

no wisdom or discernment,
no knowledge or instinct

upon which to draw and depend.
No place to stand my ground.

Can I trust You?
How to trust one thing

over another?
asks my Lord.

Why not trust everything?
Stop playing the game

and only God is left
holding the bag.

O child of God, wanting and having nothing,
leaves nothing upon which to gamble.

A living lie

Jesus said, I am the Truth.
My Master said, *I am nothing*

but a living lie ....
For the two-millenniums-old Jesus,

the tattered scriptures, the crucified Christ,
He said – *I am not the body. I am not the mind.*

For the Bhagavad Gita and the Buddha's mu,
He said – *I am not this. I am not that.*

Jesus' phrase, having become a complacency,
is rejoined by a provocative conundrum.

I am nothing, said my Lord, *but a living lie
of the truth that is Me.*

To enter the realm of Illusion (apparently)
Truth eternal must become a living lie –

not just for the Godman
but, for all God-in-human-forms.

O child of God, Meher added, ... *and unless
the lie is dead, the Truth cannot be.*

To love others

To love others, the preacher said,
we must feel others' pain

but, how might we possibly do that
unless we first feel our own?

Turn and embrace, without looking
over its shoulder, our own pain.

Breathe in the saved-up-from-childhood
darkness and ignorance, panic and dread,

just to see if we might survive.
Flight, the sum moments of our lives

might be described as, from one anesthetizing,
enisling distraction to another, inside

and outside the mind while the truth
we need face may only be shadows

flitting about the room above our crib.
Pain is real, elemental, unavoidable

but, its accompanying fear may not be –
and it is our own interior frontier

we must traverse – our cowering hearts
holding the torch, leading the way.

O child of God, to love our neighbors as ourselves
means nothing if we do not love ourselves.

The first crease

Like the first crease in the pitching distance
on the cricket field, bowler to batter

or, the line of a footrace
to evenly curb each toe –

such is the kind of scratch
we must get back to.

Eruch said to begin
by earnestly kidding yourself –

your incredulous mind
thrown under the wheels

of that terrible, redemptive law –
what you wish for, you eventually receive.

Kid yourself that He's in the chair
until His grace opens your eyes

to the presumed Reality
that it's kidding yourself

to believe the chair is empty.
Starting from scratch, score zero –

the rule-tending, scorekeeping,
handicaps and accumulations,

boundaries and demarcations
yet to come – fixed, impervious and binding.

O child of God, return to that edgeless,
quiet unknown before the first pitch is thrown.

Just God

God roused Himself from slumber
and wondered Who He is.

God is the Word (the scriptures tell us).
One extended metaphor is all of existence.

We give God our qualities –
human emotions and motives,

exploits and purposes to avoid the terrible truth
that we, also, do not know Who He is.

God is the Word
but the Word has no meaning.

Just a whimsical utterance. Just *That*. Just God.
And the resulting (to the ego, unbearable)

truth is that our brief, aspiring lives,
beyond God, have no meaning.

We likewise are just an utterance.
Just *That*. Just God.

O child of God, everything is zero.
No room for triumph or defeat.

Emptiness poised

Adam, they say, was made of spit and dust
but, suppose it was sand

processed into glass upon each arrival –
the body a lens, a window, a peephole

through which God might perceive
the world He has created

from every possible vantage point
until the doomed glass shatters,

rejoins an endless stream
of innumerable, new configurations.

Suffering comes (the Enlightened Ones say)
when we see ourselves

as the unique, fragile glass
rather than the emptiness

upon which it is poised
between God,

on the one hand,
and existence on the other.

O child of God, earnestly search for your Father
through the eye which cannot see itself.

Unsweetened lines

No sweet talk; no apologies;
not sugar-coated; hard to swallow –

though, I do wish I knew more
about the truths to which they allude.

I don't pluck them from the air,
nor from my chest or brain.

I package them best I can –
these unsweetened lines –

and serve them to each guest.
O poet, the words say, tell everyone –

kneel down and pray
in the dust from which you came.

The sugar's down there – *mixed with dust.*
There's a soft respite in the stones

on which you prostrate yourself;
nectar on the tongue in the saying of His name.

O child of God, words bitter and sweet
must be used to tell the story of love.

Words won't do

Tired of getting sucker-punched;
taken down a notch

when I lift my head too high.
Could be worse, I'm told.

Tired of going it alone; of being on alert;
navigating, calculating, daring not

take my hand off the wheel.
All for the best, the teachings say.

Painfully yearning for a breather –
a release from pain and fear.

Words won't do it. No comfort in words.
It takes a Presence. A living Presence

to shatter the solitude and loneliness –
a returning, reaffirming Presence

every time the bottom is hit,
when His name is called out –

to answer the plea
He dares not neglect.

O child of God, Meher kept silent.
You've been given enough words.

At heaven's gate

Two souls stood at heaven's gate,
the first ordered by an angel

to immediately reincarnate.
I knew him, said the remaining soul.

He was famous for his devotion.
Why was he turned away?

Attachment, the angel replied.
His days were spent in prayer, said the man.

He lived on the street, begged for his food.
Owned little more than the clothes on his back.

Filth and rags, replied the angel.
His attachment was to filth and rags,

to his empty belly, to his image
in the eyes of others, to his ideas

of what is worthy and what is worthless.
And you, sir, continued the angel,

have reached this same critical height.
What have you done to earn God's grace?

The man lowered his eyes and said nothing.
Enter paradise, said the angel, swinging wide the gate.

O child of God, when you think you've got it figured out,
be sure you do not have it figured out.

Grace and whim

Creation began on a Whim.
Is sustained on a Whim.

Periodically, the Avatar checks in
to teach us what we must do for liberation

but this time around, He chose,
by His grace, not to teach.

One terrible attribute of grace and whim –
both are beyond the grasp

of human will – devoid of rationale.
We're ever at the mercy of grace,

a mercy best described as fathomless
both for its infinite depth

and its incomprehensibility.
And our devout efforts

toward liberating ourselves
seem to be merely benign ways to serve out

the fated, inevitable terms
of our individual confinements.

O child of God, the most tenacious
of human attachments is the desire for autonomy.

Motionless and shallow

Up to my armpits in quicksand.
First thing to do is to stop

flailing about; try to stretch out
motionless and shallow on the surface,

all the while praying devoutly for help.
Meher Baba said, "Don't worry, be happy",

not because He especially wished His lovers
to be comfortable and complacent

but, because worry is *always* about Illusion.
(No one worries about Reality.)

Always for the non-existent future –
our concerns for mortality, vulnerability, pride,

pain and suffering, all of which,
according to Meher Baba, do not, in Reality, exist.

O child of God, stretch out (prayerfully) motionless
and shallow, on the treacherous surface of the great Illusion.

Where the day will take us

Harder each year, becomes the routine –
folding and unfolding myself;

reach, stretch, bend and arch. Harder still
to flex that not-the-body pertaining to me –

to keep it vital – generous and receptive.
Jesus said, become as a little child –

when I went about
where the day would take me,

shedding hierarchical impositions;
exploring the outposts and wild purlieus –

nameless and unruly; heroic and *detached*.
It's not that unmarked tablet

(lost on the way to school)
we must recover but, our *flexibility*,

our susceptibility, slipping out
of our tendencies, our utterly crushing contexts,

young and vigorous, lithesome and nimble,
adventuresome deep in our bones,

as we go about exploring the vast,
Godly paths of where the day will take us.

O child of God, are your own arrangements
superior to your Father's intentions?

The valley of the shadow

Could be like a lightning strike – a life,
intense, elemental, erratic and brief.

We seem to inch along the path,
aeons in each direction but,

outside of time, perhaps each descent –
charged with purpose, rife with destruction –

is pinpoint accurate
and, in each case, ultimately effective.

After all, we're near the apex,
the culmination of a journey.

Might we not walk now
through the valley of the shadow (of Reality),

eschewing fear *and* evil,
our earthly forays

lighting up the atmosphere with ecstatic energy
to change forever the fixed landscape below?

O child of God, you don't know truth enough
to be forlorn and disheartened.

Death poem

I hope to pen a farewell poem, jisei
(in the Zen-haiku tradition)

my very last day on earth but, I'm thinking –
why wait? This empty page tempts me

to leave it blank beneath the provocative title ...
but, that's not the story ... not the whole story.

You have given me – are giving me –
words with which to fill in the blanks,

tainted to be sure, approximated,
strained through the human brain and heart

but, divine in origin, intent and gravity.
I find my voice when You begin to speak

through my throat and fingers. O Lord,
may the last poem we write be love divine

put impossibly into words, my part being
the unread, empty spaces between the lines.

O child of God, pray your death poem to write
someday in the dust beneath your Master's feet.

www.ingramcontent.com/pod-product-compliance
Lightning Source LLC
Chambersburg PA
CBHW072000040426
42447CB00009B/1423